VIOL
WC

A PREVENT
GUID

**NEW ENGLAND INSTITUTE
OF TECHNOLOGY
LEARNING RESOURCES CENTER**

VIOLENCE IN THE WORKPLACE

A PREVENTION AND MANAGEMENT GUIDE FOR BUSINESSES

by

S. Anthony Baron, Ph.D, Psy.D

Pathfinder Publishing of California
Oxnard, CA

VIOLENCE IN THE WORKPLACE:

Published by:
Pathfinder Publishing of California
3600 Harbor Boulevard, # 82
Oxnard, CA 93035
805.984.7756

Copyright 1993 by S. Anthony Baron, Ph.D., Psy.D.
Second Printing, August 1993
Second Edition, November 2000
Library of Congress Cataloging-in-Publication Data

Baron, S. Anthony
      Violence in the workplace: a prevention and management guide for businesses/
         by S. Anthony Baron
            P. CM
Includes index
ISBN 0-934793-48-4: $24.95
ISBN 0-934793-49-2: $14.95
ISBN 0-934793-70-0: $14.95 (Canada $22.95)

1. Employee crimes. 2. Violence-Forecasting. 3. Employees-Mental health. 4. Employees--Psychology. 5. Problem employees
I. Title
HF5549.5.E43B39 1993   93-19114
658.3'8--dc20   CIP

DEDICATED

**TO THE MEMORY OF BILL HAGEN
AND
ALL THOSE WHO HAVE LOST
LOVED ONES BECAUSE OF
WORKPLACE VIOLENCE**

ACKNOWLEDGMENTS

It is of course impossible to thank all the persons who have supported and encouraged me in preparing this book. I am, however, especially indebted to Bill Hagen, a San Diego Union-Tribune newspaperman of the first rank. It was Bill and his wife, Julie, who helped me research most of the cases of workplace violence outside of California. His suggestions, editing, and rewriting of some of the chapters are deeply appreciated. Sorrowfully, Bill passed away before he was able to see the book published.

To Bobbi Baron, my wife and best friend, who spent endless hours reading the manuscript, reviewing ideas, and encouraging me to make the psychological aspects of the manuscript understandable to her colleagues in the Human Resources field, I am grateful. Thank you for your labor of love.

I wish to express my gratitude to Tom Erickson, Vice President of Human Resources at Elgar Corporation, for his friendship and assistance. He was helpful in his willingness to discuss painful memories of his workplace violence tragedy.

Paul Lawrence, Training Manager for the United States Postal Service, opened many doors at the Postal Service in research for this book and for my seminar, "Supervising the Emotionally Enraged Employee" so that I could meet their unique needs.

To my colleagues at Baron Center, Inc., I am especially

grateful for their encouragement and support.

In particular, I want to thank Dr. Sue Hoffman and Dr. Steve Albrecht. Both have made a significant contribution to the field of workplace violence prevention and I am deeply grateful for their commitment to excellence, extraordinary professional skills, and unconditional charity.

Additionally, I want to thank Muriel Housman and Jaimee Pittman for their dedication in completing the myriad of tasks that make Baron Center a great place to work. I consider all of them friends.

Finally, I am grateful to all my special "angels" whose love and encouragement are simply too great to be expressed. Without your belief in me, this book would have never happened. To God be the glory!

S. Anthony Baron, Ph.D., Psy.D.
November 1, 2000

CONTENTS

PART IV INTERVENTION

PART V CONCLUSION

FOREWORD

If you had asked me about violence in the workplace two years ago, I wouldn't have understood what you were talking about. In my 20 plus years of Human Resources experience I can't think of one physical fight I had to break up. I have worked with individuals who were pretty hot under the collar, but things were resolvable without further incident. Oh! A car was reported as having a scratch put on it by a suspected fellow employee.

June 4, 1991, I learned that I could be stalked, hunted, and killed in my office. By pure fate, luck, or whatever you call it, I was spared—but two of my friends and colleagues were murdered in cold blood in front of fellow employees. I will never be the same after that, and I believe that's true for many of my fellow employees.

The lesson I gained from this tragedy was not a new one. Companies are made up of people with all their human complexities and frailties. My job as a Human Resource professional and manager is to be sensitive to, to understand, to support, to share, to challenge, and to relate to, the individuals and the group of employees collectively. There is an innate confidence that somehow, some way, my participation will facilitate individual and group effectiveness and growth, leading to successful performance of a shared commercial enterprise.

Somehow over the 20 years, I lost sight of my job, and

I became an efficient administrator—doing what it takes to comply with laws, regulations, and sound practices.

I thought I knew Larry Hansel; I guess I just administered for him.The message in this book is to take the time—make the time—to know the people in your organization; look intently for how each individual is doing, help fellow managers and employees to be sensitive to one another, take the risk, and offer yourself to the subtle cries for help.

This guide would have been a great aid to me during our crisis in 1991: understanding post-traumatic stress, and putting all the pieces back together—or perhaps the preventive steps could have reduced the likelihood of this tragedy occurring at all. This is mandatory reading for any Human Resource professional.

This book will provide you with principles, systems, and checklists that will assure that you will not forget your job as a manager or Human Resource professional.

Tom Erickson
Vice President, Human Resources
March 3, 1993

INTRODUCTION

Violence has been a recurring nightmare in organizations throughout the United States. Any company that experiences violence in its workplace goes through profound change. Many believe that violent incidents only happen somewhere else, not to their company. Yet statistics show that what was virtually unheard of a quarter of a century ago, murder in the workplace became, at the time we initially wrote this book, one of the fastest growing types of homicide in the early 1990's. Due to increasing knowledge and intervention, workplace murder has decreased 34% from 1994 to 1998 (Bureau of Justice Statistics, Spring 2000). However, still today, the leading cause of death for women on the job is homicide and other acts of violence at work continue to increase.

In addition to the cost of violence in the workplace to employees and their families, companies also suffer costs such as interruption of business, increased legal and medical fees, and loss of productivity. Victims pay approximately $44 billion of the $57 billion in tangible non-service expenses for traditional crimes of violence. Employers pay almost $5 billion due to these crimes (U.S. News and World Report, July 1, 1996). Planning can do two things, it can prevent human suffering, and save a lot of money.

This book is a guideline for companies in the development of sound plans to help prevent and manage violent incidents. It can be used by Human Resource professionals, as well as all supervisors, managers, employees, and others who deal with clients or customers. It offers knowledge needed by employees and managers to deal with explosive situations.

It is my hope that you will learn, as I did, that it is possible to find something of great value in the midst of pain, bloodshed, and the loss of life. It is wise for every company to have a Violence Prevention and Management Plan in place. Not just management, but everyone in the workplace environment must be responsible for helping to prevent violence. I hope this book will contribute to this goal.

S. Anthony Baron, Ph.D., Psy.D.

PART I

VIOLENCE IN COMPANIES

CHAPTER 1

"THAT'S JUST LARRY"

THE ELGAR CORPORATION

The weather that morning was depressingly overcast, a reflection of Larry Hansel's mood. But there had been unmistakable psychological storm warnings long before that fateful day when Hansel walked out of the four-bedroom home he shared with his wife and two children, climbed into his blue pickup truck and drove away.

He followed a route he knew as well as he knew his way home, the same route he had followed almost every morning of the three years he had worked as an electronics technician for Elgar Corporation. But that daily drive had ended three months earlier when Hansel had been laid off "for economic reasons."

The Elgar facility is nestled in a valley that is the high-tech hub of San Diego, California. The corporation has about 300 employees engaged in the manufacture of electronic test and measurement equipment for the defense industry and power conditioning and battery backup equipment for microcomputers and computer networks. Despite annual sales of more than $40 million, executives of Elgar liked to think of the company as a "mom and pop" operation. They strove to foster a family feeling among the employees. Indeed, less than two years earlier workers who had invested in the company shared in the profits of a $40 million buyout deal for a company that had been purchased only three years earlier for $7 million.

Until recently Hansel, 41, had been a member of that "family" although, as became increasingly evident after the tragic event, he was always something of a black sheep. When he climbed into his pickup the morning of June 4, 1991, he was on a scouting expedition. His search-and-destroy mission was only hours away.

Hansel's craving for revenge may have become irrepressible in the cab of his truck as he made that familiar drive, but his explosive behavior had been building up in him for some time—for much longer than the three months since he'd lost his job. There had been signs, many of them, some as bright as flares, that Hansel was, at the very least, disturbed. His problems were not completely ignored by Elgar. Hansel was encouraged to see a counselor. But many critical signs had been either unnoticed, dismissed or excused with, "Ah, that's just Larry. Sure he's a little strange, but basically he's all right."

After the tragic incident at Elgar, others would admit that, yes, Hansel had for months made them feel increasingly uncomfortable with his unsolicited opinions about religion and politics. He seemed obsessed with both topics and was liable at any time to embark on rambling discourses, his gray eyes flashing. His views on both subjects bordered on extremism.

He was particularly fond of quoting the Old Testament prophets of doom. Politically he leaned toward Lyndon LaRouche and in 1984 even sought election as a delegate pledged to LaRouche, a far-right-wing activist who that year was seeking the Democratic presidential nomination. Hansel got 521 votes in his district, finishing near the bottom of the ballot.

Away from work there were other telltale signs. Recently Hansel had become convinced that UFOs had been landing in his backyard. He had shared this belief with friends and neighbors. A typical reaction from a neighbor and friend: "You have to understand Larry. He's just over-intelligent."

Whatever stress, real or imagined, that Hansel was suffering was undoubtedly intensified by his increasing estrangement from his family, including a wife and two children, ages 13 and 7. According to Hansel's brother-in-law, it was a "family in a crisis."

Hansel thought of himself as a survivalist. He liked the desert, camping, bike riding, and target practice. He had a sizable gun collection. He liked to dress in camouflage fatigues and was well known at a place called the Wild Geese Gun Shop, where he sometimes stood in as cashier. At the shop he became acquainted with several law enforcement officers. Said one officer of the group that gathered regularly at the shop, "They were all nice guys."

On his morning foray to Elgar, Hansel parked his pickup and walked into the building. He stopped to talk to a receptionist. He mentioned the names of three executives, casually asked if they were in the building and, if not, when they might be. He could get no definitive answer. It didn't matter. He had plenty of time. Hansel left. He would be back, very soon.

How he spent the intervening hours is uncertain, although some time was obviously required to set up a diversionary and potentially deadly facet of his scheme — planting radio-controlled bombs around the area. He also hid his mountain bike, which he would later use in his escape.

By early afternoon, Hansel was ready to return. He parked his pickup some distance from the building. Once again he walked into the lobby, this time with a bandoleer of ammunition draped over his shoulders, a shotgun held upright in one arm. He was also armed with a hit list, six names, all in a supervisorial capacity with Elgar. As Hansel once again approached the company entrance, a receptionist got a startling telephone call. "Call the police," the caller said urgently. Hansel, the caller said, was in the company's production area, and he had a shotgun. It was about 2:20 p.m.

Before the receptionist could respond, Hansel emerged from a door behind her. "Get up," he ordered. She did. Hansel leveled his shotgun at the switchboard, fired. The switchboard was destroyed. Hansel was oblivious to the fleeing, terrified receptionist. He turned toward the stairs to the second floor, where the executive offices were located. As Hansel continued relentlessly on his murderous mission, the rear of the building was rocked by explosions. He had detonated two of his radio-controlled devices. Firefighters would later find and disarm four other bombs in the area. The bombs were described as "very sophisticated devices." Also found, near a dumpster outside, were two Molotov cocktails.

Hansel reached the second floor and started down a carpeted corridor. Two men were standing near a facsimile machine, talking. One of the men was on Hansel's list. The other was an innocent bystander. Hansel shot them both. Then he wheeled and fired again, obliterating a glass wall. A man, shocked by the gunfire, darted from his nearby office, almost right into Hansel. "He looked me straight in the eye and said, 'You can go, the lucky survivor said, shaking his head in disbelief.'"

Hansel continued his prowl, then stopped and stared into an apparently deserted office. In the office, out of sight, crouched beneath a desk was another of Hansel's intended victims. For interminable, breathless moments the intended victim stared at Hansel's feet. Finally, Hansel turned and walked away, retracing his steps. He paused on the way to shoot his previous victims a second time.

On his way down the stairs, Hansel encountered another

employee who was trying to warn his fellow workers to evacuate the building. Hansel had his gun on one shoulder and was chewing gum.

The man reported, "At first I walked right past him and said, 'Hi, Larry,' I was just in shock. I thank God he didn't turn the gun on me."

Hansel walked out the back of the building "holding his shotgun, real nonchalant," another witness said. "The guy stared me down for about five seconds. Then he started to raise the shotgun. I took off."

At 2:27 p.m., San Diego police received first reports of the incident through a telephone call made from the building next door. The incident was reported as "an assault with a deadly weapon." In the confusion, the wrong address was given for Elgar Corporation. Eleven minutes later, at 2:38 p.m., police units arrived on the scene. The scene at Elgar was chaotic, as were the excited reports from witnesses. "Four people dead." "Lots of gunfire." "Explosions." The gunman was still "in the building," whereabouts unknown.

But Hansel was not in the building. He had fled on his mountain bike, shotgun strapped over a shoulder. He rode to his pickup truck, then drove away. A few hours later he walked into a Riverside County sheriff's substation in Palm Desert, about 130 miles away, and announced he had killed two men in San Diego.

****

In May 1992, less than one year after the two executives at Elgar Corporation had been murdered while they stood chatting in a second-floor corridor of the company's headquarters, Larry Hansel was in Superior Court in San Diego, California.

Among the charges that were brought against Hansel

were two counts of murder. The evidence that Hansel had fired the fatal shots was overwhelming and incontrovertible. In addition to numerous eyewitnesses, at least two of whom had themselves been threatened with the shotgun, and all of whom had seen Hansel prowling the building, there was Hansel's own admission.

"He just walked in and said he had killed two people in San Diego," a deputy recalled.

Hansel was in court this day to hear his attorney tell a judge that his client, Hansel, had been insane at the time of the slayings. Few other pleas seemed open to the hard-pressed attorney, given the weight of the evidence. In view of information about Hansel's history that had surfaced since his arrest, it was perhaps a plea not totally without merit. His client, his attorney said, had for some time been distraught, disgruntled, and unbalanced. And he had been pushed to the breaking point by the loss of his job. Other factors certainly were involved in Hansel's murderous rampage, such as an apparently deteriorating family life. But the focus of his fury was the company that had dismissed him, specifically Hansel's superiors. He made a decision to sacrifice himself for a cause against all management. As his rage festered for three months at what he perceived to be an injustice, Hansel compiled a hit list. There were six names on it, including one of his victims.

FOREWARNING

Before Hansel made his vengeful and violent visit to his former workplace, he had strewn that tragic trail with warning signs. Yet on that fateful afternoon his entrance into the facility was unobstructed. No warnings were passed along until it was too late, at least for his victims. The company had a culture that encouraged former workers and their families to visit the premises. However, this was a man who, well before he had been laid off, had made many of his fellow workers uncomfortable with his tirades about religion and politics. Complaints had been made about his behavior and were, in fact, going to be used against Hansel sometime in the near future. But economic cutbacks spared the company the onerous task of firing Hansel which, a company official said after the fact, almost certainly would have happened.

"Larry Hansel was a very capable technician," said one company executive, ironically one of the men who had been on Hansel's hit list. Because he was very capable, he continued to work. He was, however, given several warnings about his comments about religion and politics, two potentially volatile topics under any circumstances and singularly inappropriate in the workplace.

TAKE THREATS SERIOUSLY

There was a time when an upsurge in work forced one of Hansel's supervisors to assign Hansel additional duties, which would require overtime. Rather than welcome the opportunity, Hansel resented it. He considered it merely additional pressure. He mumbled something about the post office in Escondido, and how what had happened there could happen anywhere. In August, 1989, a 52-year-old career postal carrier had shot and killed two co-workers, wounded a third and then turned the gun on himself. Only later would Hansel's remarks become significant and even seem prophetic. At the time they were just another work-related gripe, of which there is never a shortage and few of which are taken seriously.

When **should** such remarks be taken seriously? What might have alerted Hansel's co-workers and supervisors to the real danger posed by Hansel's growing anger, extreme views and disorientation? Can potentially violent employees be identified? Can tragic episodes such as Hansel's be averted?

NOTES

CHAPTER 2

NATIONWIDE VIOLENCE:
WHO ARE THE PERPETRATORS?

NATIONWIDE VIOLENCE

Hansel's case is an almost perfect textbook example of an increasingly alarming kind of nationwide terrorism; violence in the workplace. It can erupt at any time, in any place, and does so with growing frequency. In the last ten years, I have personally been involved in assisting grieving families and individuals at the Columbine High School shooting and the Oklahoma City bombing. I have been asked by major hospitals, government agencies, national universities, and corporations to provide risk assessments and training programs. Our organization deals daily with disgruntled employees, intense anger issues, and ineffective leadership styles.

It was in 1992 that the Postal Service asked me to serve on the Executive Committee in Washington D.C. to develop a national training program for the USPS. At that time, the workplace violence statistics were confusing and inconsistent. One study indicated that 15 persons are murdered each month while on the job. Yet another source concluded that 1,600 homicides a year occur in the workplace.

One reason for the disparity in the figures, any one of which is startling, was that workplace violence was a new field of study, so new that there wasn't a consensus on who should be included in the toll. A man leaves his house, drives to his former place of employment and shoots and kills two former co-workers. He places the .22-caliber semiautomatic pistol against his own head and pulls the trigger. Subsequent investigation reveals that before leaving the house, he had also murdered his wife. Is she a victim of workplace violence? Is he? And so the figures fluctuate.

TRENDS

While more recent statistics indicate a slight decline in the annual number of workplace murders (Bureau of Labor Statistics, Census of Fatal Occupational Injuries reports 923 annual average workplace homicides between 1994 and 1998), research clearly shows a significant, continuing escalation in other types of violence and conflict in the workplace. The facts indicate that traditionally dangerous types of work such as police officers, bar staff, social workers, firefighters, bank tellers, and others are not the only work groups at risk. Schools, universities, and hospitals have experienced more crime. More than 7,500 cases of violent crimes were reported in the first crime reports required annually of U.S. colleges under federal law. The "National Traumatic Occupational Fatalities" (NTOF) Project reported that during 1980-1985, 13 percent of all occupational fatalities were a result of homicide. The percent of on-the-job deaths that were a result of violent crime was 12 percent for males and a stunning 42 percent for females. NTOF data only reflect deaths, not injuries, trauma or other violence in the workplace. According to statistics published by the Bureau of Labor Statistics in 1998, 12 percent of all occupational fatalities were a result of homicide. An estimated 8 percent of rapes, 7 percent of robberies, and 16 percent of all assaults occurred while victims were on duty. Although men were most likely to be attacked at work by a stranger, women were most likely to be attacked by someone they know (Bachman, 1994).

INDUSTRY

According to the Bureau of Labor Statistics, Census of Fatal Occupational Injuries, 1993-1998, the highest number of work-related homicide deaths in 1998 occurred in the retail trade (40%), with the service industry accounting for 19% of the deaths, and public administration another 13%. The occupational group with the highest number of work-related homicides was the service occupation workers (19.3%) with the sales workers reporting another 16.5%. Executive administrators and managers accounted for 14.3%. Businesses and corporations that have never before been concerned about workplace violence are being confronted with this issue. Violence can erupt in situations involving an employee angry with management or from outside clients, customers or vendors. "Murder On the Job," a 1992 article by P. Stuart in **Personnel Journal**, lists 28 incidents of murder in the workplace that occurred between March 31, 1986, and November 14, 1991. In these 28 incidents, the death toll reached 161, and 56 were injured. The prevalence of the problem of workplace violence obviously makes one ask the haunting questions: Why? What impact does this have on the businesses involved? Can the reasons be identified, and what can be done to prevent this violence? Consider the potential impact, both financial and psychological, that a violent incident in the workplace can set in motion on the victims, their families, co-workers, and friends.

These figures do not even include the untold numbers of incidents of workplace violence which do not result in fatalities—for example, physical or sexual assault, which injure but do not kill, and acts of sabotage against equipment, materials, or property. Perhaps most insidious is another kind of violence in the workplace—psychological or verbal abuse. This is the kind of "violence" which does no apparent bodily harm, but which can, nevertheless, erode an employee's mental health, a company's health, vitality, and profits. Examples are threats, verbal abuse, demeaning or belittling statements, and ridicule .

On some issues there is an almost unanimous consensus. Workplace violence is nationwide. And neither a state-of-the-art security system nor the most advanced psychological expertise can guarantee an end to it. Together, though, preventive measures can reduce the risks. Predictive and preventive strategies can alert and avert, particularly when encompassing the use of mental health providers, the company's Human Resource Department and targeted training programs.

A RECURRENT NATIONAL NIGHTMARE

EXAMPLES

Quintessence Building Maintenance Co.

Thirty-year-old Jonathan Daniel D'Arcy, a janitor, was angry over the late payment of a $150 check. In January of 1993, he approached the receptionist at the firm on the second floor of the company's Spanish-style office about 8:30 a.m., asking to see the bookkeeper. "I want to see Kari now," he said. When the receptionist asked the bookkeeper if she wanted to see D'Arcy she was waved away. "I don't want to see him now," Kari said, "I'm very busy." D'Arcy pushed past the receptionist and went into the bookkeeper's office, yelling, "I want my . . . money." He was carrying a cup full of bluish-green liquid which he threw over the bookkeeper's head and body. The receptionist said she did not see what ignited the liquid, but suddenly there were flames coming from the room and she saw D'Arcy flee. Detectives believe that he ignited the liquid with a lighter. The bookkeeper, a 42-year-old mother of two teenagers died nine hours later after suffering burns over 95 percent of her body.

Jonathan D'Arcy was arrested after the attack in a nearby parking lot. He was an outside contract janitor hired occasion-

28

ally by Quintessence to clean offices. Police said D'Arcy, a tall, thin man with a criminal record for burglary and domestic violence had a problem over "a check that had not been paid." A salesman for the company said that D'Arcy was a man quick to lose his temper. "He was rather highstrung, but a great worker," he said. The $150 check owed to the janitor was on the bookkeeper's desk and was probably burned in the fire.

Could the company have been forewarned of this tragedy? Is there anything that could have been done to prevent it?

Texas

"There is no factual, rational, or logical explanation for this act of criminal lunacy," Mi-T-Fine car wash owner Luke Ramsey said in a statement after six of his employees had been gunned down by a former employee. On Monday, March 21, 2000 Robert Wayne Harris, according to his admission to police, entered the car wash and shot six of his former co-workers as they were preparing to begin the workday, killing five of them early that morning. Before he could escape he was discovered by an employee who was arriving for work. Harris had been terminated the Friday before after being arrested for exposing himself to customers at the car wash. On Sunday he was released on bail. Harris was a convicted burglar and a suspect in the November 1999 disappearance of a woman who lived near the car wash.

Hawaii

A 40-year-old Xerox copy repairman entered his workplace with a 9-mm semiautomatic handgun and fired at least 20 times killing two co-workers in an office and five in a conference room. Prosecutors say Byran Uyesugi, a 15-year employee of the company, murdered his co-workers and supervisors as they were gathering for a meeting to discuss his job performance. He escaped in a company van and then surrendered after a five-hour standoff with police.

At Uyesugi's home police found 11 handguns, five rifles and two shotguns. Uyesugi had been a sharpshooter on his high school rifle team. According to the Honolulu Police Department Uyesugi indicated on a 1994 gun permit application that he had previous mental problems. He was told the application could only be processed when he submitted a doctor's note stating that he was mentally fit to own a firearm. The note was never produced. In 1985 he was convicted of drunken driving. He attended an anger-management course to erase a criminal damage charge for kicking an office elevator door in 1993. Three court-appointed examiners said Uyesugi suffered from schizophrenia and delusions of persecution. In preparing for trial, Uyesugi told medical experts that he felt his co-workers were harassing him. "They were just messing with me too much."

Tennessee

In October 1999 six-year veteran firefighter Fred Williams, 41, was arrested after a domestic disturbance involving his fiancée. He later married her on Valentine's Day but was estranged from her shortly after. The court date regarding the domestic violence incident was set for March 16, 2000. In early March he moved in with his wife once again. He took a leave of absence for "employee assistance" and returned to work on Monday, March 6 but left early stating he was ill and did not report for his shifts on Tuesday or Wednesday.

On Wednesday, March 8th, firefighters responded to the alarm of a burning home – it was the home of Fred Williams. As they prepared to subdue the blaze Williams burst from his garage screaming, "Get away! Get away!" and firing a shotgun. Two firefighters and a sheriff's deputy were killed in the ambush, and Williams' wife was killed.

Wisconson

from which he had been discharged only hours earlier, sought out the man he held responsible, and shot him to death with a .22-caliber pistol. The gunman was later arrested.

Beck had been on medications for more than a year to help him with suicidal depression. His father had saved him from a suicide attempt the previous year. Beck had been cleared by his psychiatrist to return to work from a four-month medical leave less than two weeks before his angry, violent attack on the lottery officials. Police found that he had a collection of weapons including two semiautomatic assault weapons.

A New York Times News Service article reported that lottery sales representative John Krinjak noticed that Beck began changing the previous summer. "He became visibly withdrawn into himself," Krinjak recalled. "He took on a severe look, an angry look. He looked like he had lost weight and gotten pale." It was common knowledge that Beck was angry with management.

One employee said that shortly after Beck arrived at work that fatal day he appeared to be "ticked off" at one of the supervisors over a work grievance. He then stabbed the supervisor and moved on methodically pursuing and shooting his other victims several times with a semiautomatic handgun. "He could have gotten any of us, but he knew who he wanted to get," said Karen Kalandyk, a supervisor who sat next to one of his victims as he said, "Bye, bye," and fired three lethal shots. "He just lowered the gun and walked away. I made eye contact, and his eyes were dead." Of his targets she said, "They were the people who had the power in the lottery. They were the ones who had turned down his promotion."

As police approached, Beck lifted his pistol to his head and fired his last two shots.

In Wisconsin, a man returned to the fast-food franchise

Maryland

In Maryland, a bank employee carrying a black athletic bag took an elevator to the seventh floor and, as the elevator doors slid open, removed from the bag a .38- caliber revolver. He shot and killed three co-workers. Another was shot in the face but survived. The bank employee then fatally shot himself in the head.

New Jersey

In New Jersey, a recently discharged postal clerk invaded a tranquil suburb, broke into the home of his former supervisor and shot her to death. He also killed her boyfriend. He left the house and, armed with what would later be described as "an arsenal of weapons," returned to the post office at which he had recently worked. There he shot and killed two mail handlers, then surrendered to a police SWAT team.

California

In California, a man fired less than two weeks earlier, his appeal for reinstatement rejected after a grievance hearing, drew a .38-caliber handgun from his person, shot and killed a company labor representative, then shot another company official in the back of the head, miraculously not fatally. The gunman threatened suicide but was later arrested.

U.S. Air - California

David Burke, 35, father of seven children and a U.S. Air Agent, was fired based on evidence that he had stolen $69 from flight cocktail receipts. Burke asked for understanding but Raymond Thompson, a Customer Service Manager, made the decision to fire him based on company policy.

In November, 1987, Burke retaliated for the loss of his job. He was aware that Ray Thompson was aboard flight 1771 to San Francisco and bought a ticket on the same flight. Being familiar with airport procedures, Burke was able to hide a Smith & Wesson .44 magnum revolver. He cleared security. When the plane was over San Luis Obispo County, Burke shot Thompson, the pilot and co-pilot. The plane crashed halfway to its destination.

Forty-three passengers were killed on this flight, including Thompson and Burke. The FBI, during the investigation at the scene, found a note, gun and six empty casings. The note read, "I asked for some leniency for my family. . . well, I got none. And you'll get none."

Florida -Customer Hostility
On June 18, 1991, eight employees at General Motors Acceptance Corporation in Jacksonville, Florida, were killed and five wounded because the company repossessed a customer's vehicle. Angry at the lack of response he felt he was getting from the company, and his own poor financial position, the customer used a .30-caliber semiautomatic rifle to get even. He then turned the rifle on himself, dying immediately.

Montreal, Canada
In Montreal, a university professor enraged by a dispute over tenure, returned to the school, shot and killed a fellow teacher and wounded a school administrator.

Strathfield, Australia
On August 17, 1991, an unemployed male stabbed a teenage girl to death before entering the shopping plaza with an automatic rifle killing five people and wounding eight others. He died at the scene after turning the weapon on himself.

Alberta, Canada
On July 3, 1991, in Edmondton, Alberta, the Canadian-

based Vipond Sprinkler Company Ltd. suffered the loss of one employee who was killed by a jealous husband who believed the employee was having an affair with his wife.

A DIFFERENT TYPE OF PERPETRATOR
Los Angeles, California
Although the usual perpetrator of violence in the workplace is a male, there have been incidents involving females. In the Los Angeles County Department of Children's Services in January, 1993, a female social worker who had been fired from her job in Santa Fe Springs 12 months previously, walked into her former office unimpeded and shot a supervisor who participated in the decision to let her go. The victim was severely wounded and the female perpetrator surrendered at the San Bernardino County Sheriff's station about three hours after the incident.

Bennington, Vermont
On October 25, 1991, Elizabeth Teague, a female employee unhappy with her treatment at work, opened fire with a 9-mm pistol at the Eveready Battery Company in Bennington, Vermont. Her target was the plant manager. He died. She critically wounded two other employees after attempting to set the plant on fire.

NO ORGANIZATION IS IMMUNE
The above incidents are a random and almost microcosmic sampling. The list of such incidents of violence in the workplace grows with frightening regularity. These incidents serve to dispel at least one dangerous and common presumption: "It can't happen here." It can and does happen anywhere, at anytime, in major cities, in small towns, in large businesses or industries, in "mom and pop" operations, in hospitals, even on college campuses. And the perpetrators can be as psychologically diverse as Larry Hansel, whose symptoms were as

obvious as flashing neon, or John Taylor, the "model employee" (case in Chapter 3).

As horrible as this increasingly recurrent national nightmare is, there's also a hidden horror to be considered. These tragedies are happening in the workplace, traditionally considered a haven second perhaps only to the home.

Only a few decades ago such an outburst of individual violence in the workplace would have been considered unthinkable. The emotionally enraged employee was a relatively unknown and largely ignored factor. Not that the good old days were as idyllic as our memories. There was probably as much griping about "this lousy job" and "that lousy manager" then as now. Griping is indigenous to work. Always has been, always will be.

But as the pace of life and the standard of living have accelerated, fueled by a technological revolution, so have the stresses. Financial stress. Emotional stress. Family stress. Professional stress. Life suddenly has become more competitive, challenging, and daunting. The key to keeping up in a continually more hurried society is one's job. Loss of a job can be devastating and unbearably traumatic.

"I feel pretty bad about what happened," Robert Mack of General Dynamics said a few days after he'd shot and killed one official and seriously wounded another. "But I done what I done. That's over with." And, he would rationalize, it wasn't entirely his fault. "They took everything I had, everything, I'd worked for," he said.

Mack, like a shockingly growing number in the work force, had gone beyond griping. He'd become a walking, ticking time bomb. But his explosion into violence, as with most similar cases, had been preceded by warning signs. His frequent absences and constant tardiness were two of them.

WHO ARE THE VIOLENT ONES?

RED FLAGS AND WARNING SIGNS

In sketching a psychological profile of an emotionally enraged employee with the potential for violence, one starting place is a review of the psychological/behavioral criteria frequently associated with individuals who become violent. Almost without fail the violent employee will fall within one or more of these groups:

1. History of Violence. A history of violence is the best predictor of violence. It overshadows all others in the area of prediction. The probability of future crime increases with each prior criminal act. Whether it is a domestic history of physical and verbal abuse during adulthood, or a lifestyle of antisocial activities, such as membership in gangs, violence will usually follow unless there is treatment. Individuals who have a developmental history of violence, i.e., were abused as children, are also more likely to be violent. Violence breeds violence.

2. Psychosis. In lay language, psychosis is simply a loss of contact with reality. Psychoses include schizophrenia, major affective disorders and paranoid states. Persons with psychosis have a thought disorder that is often reflected in loose associations in their conversations, flat facial expressions and extreme ambivalence. Additionally, schizophrenics will manifest hallucinations, poor insight, verbalize and argue with their thoughts, and often express bizarre, sometimes nihilistic delusions. For example, an individual may believe a part of his/her body is no longer present or that all the emotions and motor activity is controlled by someone else. Individuals with this disorder may even believe a UFO has landed in their backyard.

Major affective disorders may also be characterized by a loss of contact with reality, but primarily they involve a mood disorder. This disorder may be accompanied by severe depression. More will be discussed later on depression.

The paranoid or delusional disorder is a third division of psychosis. The popular concept of a paranoid is the person who is convinced that someone, perhaps even everyone, is out to get him or her. But there are also other manifestations of paranoia. For example, grandiose paranoids may believe they have insight that no one else has. Some see them as delusional leaders of religious cults, like Rev. Jim Jones convincing his followers to join him in a suicide pact. David Koresh and his religious followers in March 1993, caused a national sensation when they held off authorities in a shoot-out near Waco, Texas. Four Federal officers were killed. Others see Jones and Koresh as having character or personality disorders in full control of their sensibilities and awareness of right and wrong.

The jealous and persecutory types are two other types of the paranoid disorders. Both types may resort to violence against those they believe are doing them harm. In the jealousy type, a person is irrationally convinced that his or her lover has been unfaithful. This type may demand restrictive rules in talking to the opposite sex and may follow the lover without his/ her knowledge. Physically attacking the lover because of unreliable evidence is not uncommon.

The persecutory type is the most common type of the delusional disorders. These individuals have a long history of resentment toward a person or organization they feel has slighted them in the past. They will have a tendency to exaggerate the misdeeds. This person will make many attempts to "right the wrong" through legal action or harassment measures. The persecutory type must be taken seriously because they have the ability for violence.

Regardless of the paranoia, projection seems to be the primary defense mechanism of these individuals. Therefore, they will focus much of their problems and unhappiness on others, such as a supervisor. Typical clues to disturbance are:

"I know they bug the phones around here. Joe is after me. He doesn't like me and he wants me out."

Delusions, mood swings, depression, or paranoia—their signs may be subtle or blatant. They should all be taken seriously.

Most clinicians think Hansel falls into the psychotic category (as demonstrated by his extreme views, hallucinations, and delusions about UFOs). It's possible, perhaps even likely, that Hansel fits into more than one category. When an employee **does** fit more than one category, there is heightened potential for violence.

3. Romance Obsession (Erotomania). This category can fall into the third division of psychosis, but the increase of this type of violence at the workplace needs to be addressed separately. What is particularly unnerving in this type of delusional disorder is that the fixated object (your employee) may be totally unaware of the high degree of attraction. This is not a sexual attraction. The erotic delusion is idealized romantic love, a bonding of almost spiritual dimensions. The fixated object may have a great deal of contact with the individual or none at all at first. Generally, the fixated object is at a higher social level, either by title, appearance, social status or financial condition. The conduct of the erotomic type is not unusual or bizarre other than this one area. Stalking, spying, visits, gifts, love letters, taping conversations, and phone calls are common.

Laura Black finally filed a temporary restraining order against Richard Farley, former co-worker and unemployed computer technician, after almost three years of romantic harassment. Farley could not stand the suffering "she had put him through" and entered his former workplace. Firing over 110 rounds of ammunition, he killed seven individuals and wounded three others. Laura Black, although wounded, survived.

The prevalence of erotomania is seen with private citizens and public celebrities. Tatiana Tarasoff, a UCLA coed, was stabbed to death after rejecting the consistent advances over time of Prosenjit Poddar. He did not want anyone else to have her. A famous case of a public celebrity murder is the death of 21-year-old Becky Schaeffer, star of the situational comedy, "My Sister Sam," at the hands of an obsessive fan Robert Bardo in 1986.

4. Chemical Dependence. Alcohol and certain drugs agitate, create paranoia and cause aggressive behavior. Although some drugs are more dangerous than others, most of them have the capacity to interfere dramatically with reasoning ability, with social inhibition, and with the ability to distinguish right from wrong. The result is that an individual who may have been marginal is pushed over the edge.

5. Depression. Depression is the most common symptom treated by counselors. Finding hope and meaning in life's darkest shadow is very difficult, sometimes impossible. Almost one in seven depressives will commit a violent act on themselves or on others up to and including suicide and/or homicide.

Signs of Depression include:

- "I just don't care anymore. What difference does it make?" (or similar expressions of despair)
- A slowed work pace
- Perpetual blank, sad, or frowning expression
- Self-destructive behavior
- Distractibility and sluggish decision-making
- Increased apathy; lack of motivation
- Withdrawing socially
- Unrealistic expectations
- Excessive self-condemnation
- Feelings of hopelessness
- Sense of helplessness
- Inappropriate guilt or shame
- Unkempt physical appearance

6. The Pathological Blamer. The external world is the reason for their problems. Those in this category accept no responsibility for their actions. Does the employee admit to wrongdoing and take responsibility for behavior or does he/she blame the organization, system or other people? "Those guys did me wrong—and they're gonna pay for it."

7. Impaired Neurological Functioning. Impaired neurological functioning reduces the capacity for impulse control. Individuals include those who were hyperactive as children, those who have brain injuries, abnormal EEGs or other subtle neurological disorders. They are more prone to aggression as they are less capable of inhibiting themselves than the average person in a similar situation.

8. Elevated Frustration with the Environment. Important outside variables to evaluate include the family environment, peer environment and job environment. A disturbance in one or more of these support systems may trigger violent behavior.

9. Interest in Weapons. When assessing an employee regarding his/her potential for violence, ownership of a gun or gun collection, fascination with weapons, and shooting skills are significant indicators to consider. Employees should be advised to inform management of any weapon brought into the workplace.

10. Personality Disorders. Personality has been defined as "consistent human behavior patterns within the individual." These patterns are lifelong in how we view, think, relate, and perceive life. Our personality has a tremendous impact on our relationships at home or at work. When these personality patterns become inflexible, impaired, and unhealthy, the traits become disorders and can reduce effectiveness in relating to others. Two such personality disorders will be discussed because of their relationship toward workplace violence.

The Antisocial Personality Disorder. Behaviorists would prefer the word "sociopath" to describe these individuals. This disorder is more common in males than females. People with this disorder tend to be irritable and aggressive with repeated track records for fighting outside the home and domestic violence inside the home. They are not opposed to harassing others, stealing, or destroying property. They have little regard for the truth, are impulsive in action, and probably own a weapon.

Generally, antisocial individuals will have little remorse about wrongdoing and justify their violent behavior. Not surprisingly, the individual will not have a long-lasting, warm, and responsible relationship with family or friends. Antisocial-personality individuals will have a history of quitting jobs without having another position available, or may be unemployed for six months or more even if they were offered employment. When they are employed, it will not be unusual to have frequent absences from work without justified explanation.

Borderline Personality Disorder The essential feature is instability and the lack of proper boundaries. You can observe the instability in interpersonal relationships, self- image, and self-mutilating behavior. There may be uncertainty for this individual concerning career choice, value system, long term goals, and/or sexual orientation.

This individual experiences severe mood shifts with inappropriate anger often displayed in repeated fights. Like the antisocial behavior, this individual is very impulsive and can be easily irritated. Excellent manipulators of people, the borderline personality individual may fear a real or imagined abandonment from others. They are not opposed to making suicidal threats to avoid loss. The borderline-personality, much like the self-absorbed narcissistic personality, are preoccupied with self and will use people to achieve their purposes.

A Final Note: Trust your judgment and senses. Dr. Robert C. Bransfield, Associate Director of Psychiatry at the Riverview Medical Center in Red Bank, New Jersey, states, "The gut feeling that one gets when talking to people should be respected. If one feels that someone is dangerous, that person should be considered dangerous."

Based on these criteria, Hansel couldn't have been any more obvious as a potential source of danger and violence if he'd been ticking. He was very much an armed but as yet unexploded bomb. He snugly and securely fit into three categories—the psychotic, the historically violent, and the blamer. And given the state of his family life, described by his brother-in-law as "in crisis," which was exacerbated by his unemployed status, he probably also qualified as severely depressed.

Violence had always been on at least the fringes of Hansel's life, as evidenced by his gun collection, his attraction to camouflage fatigues, and his fascination with the Wild Geese Gun Shop. There were other signs, such as his sick joke, often told to co-workers, that Ezekial of the Old Testament really meant, "E.Z. Kill." He spoke with relish to fellow employees about other murders in the workplace. As for blame, Hansel had those six names on his hit list. They were the cause of his troubles. They would pay. One of them did. So did an innocent bystander. The toll could have been worse, considering the explosive devices he had planted in the area.

But none of these early signals was perceived as a warning. What could have led to an "alert and avert" strategy for the organization instead was brushed aside as, "Oh, that's just Larry . . . no cause for real alarm." Alert and avert. With Hansel, the system either broke down or was not yet in place and fully operational.

"Without being critical of the organization," a San Diego police official said in the aftermath of that afternoon of terror, "several employees were aware of Hansel's previous idiosyncratic behavior, unpredictability, and threats that went unreported." Recognizing and providing help to employees under unusual stresses in their lives is as important as providing physical and medical care. More emphasis on psychological assistance is needed if for no other reason than, in the long run, it will save the corporation money and possibly save lives.

VIOLENCE TAKES MANY FORMS

LEVEL ONE:

- Refuses to cooperate with immediate supervisor
- Spreads rumors and gossip to harm others
- Consistently argues with co-workers
  Belligerent toward customers/clients
- Constantly swears at others
- Makes unwanted sexual comments

LEVEL TWO:

- Argues increasingly with customers, vendors, co-workers and management
- Refuses to obey company policies and procedures
- Sabotages equipment and steals property for revenge
- Verbalizes wishes to hurt co-workers and/or management
- Sends sexual or violent notes to co-workers and/or management
- Sees self as victimized by management (me against them)

LEVEL THREE:

- Frequent displays of intense anger resulting in:
  Recurrent suicidal threats
  Recurrent physical fights
  Destruction of property
  Utilization of weapons to harm others
  Commission of murder, rape, and/or arson

NOTES

CHAPTER 3

"HE WAS A MODEL EMPLOYEE"

THE ORANGE GLEN POST OFFICE

No one thought it was unusual when John M. Taylor arrived that Thursday morning at the Orange Glen Post Office a half-hour before his shift was scheduled to begin.

"Just like John," fellow workers would say later. "He'd rather be a half-hour early than a minute late." Such was his dedication and pride in his work, and had been for the 27 years he'd worked for the U.S. Postal Service. Taylor's diligence hadn't gone unnoticed. Over the years he'd received several awards and commendations. Only recently, Taylor, 51, had been selected to receive a quarterly performance award. He'd asked that the award be given to someone else because he'd won it several times previously. That, too, was "just like John", one of the traits that made him perhaps the most likable of all the employees at the small postal station 35 miles north of San Diego.

"He was unfailingly friendly and congenial, always had a smile on his face," one of Taylor's supervisors recalled. "If you were to make a composite of a model employee, you'd come up with John Taylor."

The ever-present smile was missing, however, when

Taylor walked into the building on the morning of August 10, 1989. One of Taylor's fellow workers was so surprised by Taylor's uncustomary grim visage that he scarcely noticed the handgun Taylor carried at his side. "He didn't have any emotion," the witness said. "He was stern-faced. That wasn't like John at all."

Taylor walked past the man and approached two other co-workers, one of whom was a close personal friend. The two men, police theorized, probably assumed Taylor was going to join them at a picnic table on the loading dock for coffee, a cigarette, and some aimless talk before punching in on the time clock. It was a morning ritual.

On this morning, with no warning, Taylor shot both men to death. As the police would learn later, it was the continuation of a murderous rampage that had begun a short time earlier in Taylor's brown stucco home, less than a mile from Taylor's workplace. In his home was the body of Taylor's wife. He had shot and killed her before going to work for the last time. The carnage wasn't over.

Taylor had taken with him a box of 100 bullets for his .22-caliber semiautomatic pistol, which he would reload at least once. Taylor walked away from the victims, entered a side door and began firing again, apparently randomly. He shot at some co-workers, bypassed others.

"I'd just walked back to check on something when John walked through the side door," a co-worker said. "I said good morning and then I heard a pop. Only then did I notice he had a gun in his hand. The second shot went through my left arm, but, to tell you the truth, I didn't even know I'd been shot until I felt the blood on my arm. I ran for the front door and another bullet passed by me. I ran next door to a restaurant and told them to call the police. Then I sat down outside and thought, not John Taylor. Why is he doing this?"

The first indication one of the postal station's supervisors had of the still unfolding tragedy was when he glanced out of his office and saw Taylor's latest victim hurrying toward him, his arm oozing blood. The wounded man said to the supervisor, "Don't go out there. He's got a gun."

The supervisor ignored the warning. "I walked out of my office," he said, "and John pointed the gun toward me. But then he said, 'I'm not going to shoot you.' He fired the gun, but away from me. I went back to my office, closed the door and called 911."

Taylor walked to a drinking fountain and accidentally dropped an ammunition clip and some loose bullets on the floor. As he bent to retrieve them he locked eyes with another employee, who said he had mistaken the sound of gunfire for plastic mail trays hitting the floor and was still unaware of what was going on.

"He looked at me, but it was like he didn't even see me," the man said. "He looked dazed. Then he walked right by me and stopped about five feet away. Then he turned and looked at me again. Then he turned away and started walking again."

Taylor walked right past another man.

"He didn't threaten me," the man said, "just walked right by me without saying a word. He headed toward the other end of the building. The gun was still in his hand. Right about then someone started yelling to clear the building. Then Taylor raised the gun shoulder high, like you'd do at a target range, getting ready for your next shot."

Police estimated that by this time Taylor had fired as many as 20 shots in the building. He would fire one more, into his right temple. As Taylor's body crumpled in a far corner of the building, unspent ammunition spilled from his pockets. The gun was still clutched in his hand.

THE AFTERMATH

Years after the horror at Orange Glen, many of those most profoundly affected were still trying to piece it together, still groping for answers. Mention of John Taylor's name conjured up responses from co-workers such as "congenial," "friendly," and "personable." Supervisors recalled Taylor as "a diligent worker" and "very service-oriented, a man who wanted to take care of business, get the job done first, a man who set high standards for himself, an excellent employee." Friends and neighbors remembered the Taylors as "very friendly, a nice couple. They had lots of friends. They went out a lot, dancing and things like that. They had people over to their home often."

A friend who had known Taylor for 15 years said he couldn't recall ever seeing Taylor at a social affair without his wife. Another friend said, "I know they loved each other very much. He called her 'Poopsie.'" On the morning of August 10, 1989, John Taylor shot his beloved wife twice in the head as she lay in their bed, then left his well-kept home and added another bloody episode to the ongoing and rapidly growing tragedy of violence in the workplace.

John Taylor remained an enigma to his co-workers. On the surface Taylor seems to defy psychological profiling, which doesn't lessen the continuing anguish of a postal service official who liked Taylor and thought he knew him well. "Hardly a day goes by," he said, "that I don't ask myself whether I missed something, whether we all missed something. Were there warning signs? But John was always such an easygoing guy. He was never belligerent or insubordinate. A 'go with the flow' kind of guy."

Said another co-worker unable to comprehend what had happened: "None of it figures. John knew those people, was friendly with them. They'd sit out there every morning and chat. And John, he never voiced a complaint as far as I know, not to anyone about anything. The rest of us, we'd always have something to gripe about. But John—John was just too nice to gripe about anything. That's what makes it all even more horrible and frightening. My God. John Taylor? Who's next?"

PERSONAL STRESS

But subsequent investigation disclosed that although Taylor's facade of normalcy was nearly flawless, certainly in the workplace, there were signals of potential trouble. Several people who knew Taylor, personally and professionally said after the tragedy that yes, they knew or suspected that Taylor had a drinking problem. But since it apparently didn't affect his performance and since he was "such a nice guy," everyone was reluctant to make an issue of it.

And in the days preceding the killings those warning signals intensified. Taylor had uncharacteristically begun grumbling about dissatisfaction at home. His 22-year-old stepson, his wife's son by a prior marriage, had moved into the Taylor house and wasn't working.

"That would have bothered John, perhaps more than most other people, because he had a very strong work ethic," a friend said. "He was bothered by what he considered widespread erosion of that work ethic, although he certainly didn't harp on it. He was also dismayed over what he considered a diminishing sense of camaraderie at work. He thought it was because of the changes in personnel over the previous two or three years, primarily in management. But he targeted no managers. No managers were shot."

Two days before Taylor would embark on this murderous mission, he would sit in on a discussion among some of his co-workers about the August 20, 1986, massacre in the Edmond, Oklahoma, Post Office. A part-time mail carrier shot and killed 14 employees, then killed himself.

"That wasn't the topic of the conversation," an employee at Orange Glen said. "It just came around to that, you know what I mean? And then someone wondered what could have happened to make a guy go berserk like that. And then someone said, 'job stress.' And we all laughed at that. John, too. He was a happy-go-lucky guy, never got mad about anything."

At the close of what would be his last day of work, Taylor said he was leaving, that there wasn't enough mail to keep everyone busy.

"I figured he was just being sarcastic," a co-worker said, "because there was a ton of mail in there."

Taylor's offhand, parting remark could well have been a final manifestation of multiple pressures that had been building in him for some time. His home life had of late become less tranquil than it had been. Another stress would be his perception that work was not as satisfying as it once had been, that personnel and procedures were changing for the worse rapidly. Indeed, the postal service had undergone more change in the last decade than in all the previous years of its existence. And other changes, profound changes, were not only inevitable, but also imminent.

Hovering over all employees, including Taylor, who was three years from being eligible for retirement, was the specter of advanced automation and an attendant loss of jobs. Postal service authorities maintained that reductions in the work force would come about largely through attrition. In any case, it's highly unlikely that Taylor, with his seniority and his glowing record, would have been affected. But it's just as unlikely, analyzing Taylor's state of mind in retrospect, that he would or could have arrived at such a conclusion.

PARANOIA

Perhaps the most telltale sign that Taylor was a disturbed man was his recent claims that he had been finding sums of money along his route and his occasionally voiced suspicion that he was being "set up" by postal inspectors. He was being watched, he thought, to see how he would handle the situation. He apparently was not at all soothed by assurances from management that such was definitely not the case, that he was a highly valued and trusted employee. Such a display of paranoia from a "model employee" was so startling that a possible course of action, or treatment, had to be evaluated. Before any recommendations had been arrived at, Taylor reached his own deadly decision.

Whatever pressures Taylor was under, real or imagined, the probability is that they would have festered within him. Taylor was an almost prototypical example of a benign personality, and one of the most powerful traits of such personalities is an overriding desire, an urgent need, for harmony. "Go along to get along." "Don't rock the boat." But there is a psychological downside to the quest for harmony. It prohibits the expression of emotions such as anger or frustration and these repressed feelings fuel resentment.

ENSUING TRAUMA

Years after the tragedy, a good, decent and compassionate man, an intelligent man, a man who had known Taylor for 15 years, sat in his office and tortured himself with the tough questions. Was the man he had known for so long sending out signals? Was he sending out a silent plea? Should the Human Resources Department and the Employee Assistance Program have been alerted? Could the tragedy have been averted?

"I keep telling myself, based on what I know now," the man said, "that what happened must have been personally motivated as opposed to work related. It's some consolation, but there will always be doubts and questions. But I'll tell you this. What happened has changed all of us. It's changed the employees' perception of management. And, certainly, in my case, it's changed management's perception of the employees. I think communication between management and employees (and here I'm not speaking just for myself) has become more personable. I think we all listen better. I'd say my job is now 80 percent people, 20 percent mail. Before that day I'd say it was maybe 40/60. And I think that's a change for the better."

THE NEED FOR COMMUNICATION
TAKING THREATS SERIOUSLY

The example of John M. Taylor, a man who had been perceived as a model employee, points up the importance for companies and organizations to have a clear written policy regarding the "chain of command" for communicating **ALL** threats of violence. Details should include what actions will be taken at all levels of management so that threats are properly evaluated and not disregarded or discounted at a lower managerial level. The plan should detail who will be used to evaluate the situation and the credibility of the threat. Employees should be informed of the importance of reporting and following the established guidelines. The method of reporting should provide confidentiality for the person reporting.

It is important that senior management take seriously all comments from Human Resource professionals and other employees concerning potential violence. In their fast-paced, task-oriented world of business, executives are often not close enough to employees to make an accurate assessment of the immediate and long-term danger of potential violence. Human Resources should be a trusted ally and important resource for valuable information.

STATE LAWS
In addition, employers should be familiar with and use state laws that prohibit certain forms of threats. Most states have laws pertaining to terroristic threatening and most permit a mental examination under certain conditions. Under these laws, a person may be involuntarily hospitalized if he/she poses a danger to self or others.

NOTES

CHAPTER 4

"LATE AGAIN"

WARNING SIGNS AND SIGNALS

GENERAL DYNAMICS

For a man who had frequently been heard to proclaim that his job was his life, Robert Earl Mack's approach to a company hearing that would determine his future in that job was rather cavalier.

The hearing had been scheduled for 1:00 p.m. on January 24, 1992, in a conference room in a General Dynamics plant in San Diego, California. Among the issues to be addressed was Mack's repeated tardiness, particularly over the past year. Mack was 40 minutes late for a meeting which, in a sense, was his court of final appeal.

Nine days earlier Mack, 42, had been fired by the company for which he had worked 25 years, ever since he'd dropped out of high school. Among the reasons for the termination were frequent unexcused absences in addition to the constant tardiness. Until the last year or so, neither had been typical of Mack, whose performance record had been acceptable. He had long since, in fact, been given top secret clearance, and at the time of his dismissal held the position of "production distribution analyst." What he did, he said, was track lost documents on the cruise missile line, ensuring both the security of the project and cost control.

"I enjoyed my job," he said later. "I loved my job. That's all I lived for, was to go to work and come home."

His claim was supported by numerous work-related books found in his home, including instruction manuals dating back to 1968. The house was the same one Mack had lived in since 1969, even after his wife and three children left after a divorce in 1977. But in all the years he'd lived there, Mack had never become active in neighborhood activities. Part of the reason, he said, was fear of compromising his top-secret clearance. "I couldn't go out and mingle with the outside public world," he said. "Everything I did was secret, secret, secret."

Waiting for Mack in the conference room were his former supervisor and a company labor negotiator. There were also three union representatives who would argue on Mack's behalf. As Mack approached the conference room, two things were different, one noticeable, one not. For the first time in 25 years, he was wearing a visitor's badge. And concealed in his clothing was a .38-caliber handgun.

Less than an hour after Mack's arrival, the company and the union agreed to a recess. They also agreed to meet again in a week. The union representatives said they were pleased with the way the meeting had gone and that they were convinced Mack had been fired without just cause. While Mack slumped in a chair in a room he later recalled as "hot and stuffy," his former supervisor and the company labor negotiator stepped out into a company courtyard. Mack got out of his chair and walked toward a drinking fountain. He later said he couldn't remember whether he drank from the fountain. Nor does he remember following the two men into the courtyard. There were about 20 other employees in the courtyard. Nearby were several hundred other employees lined up at time clocks, waiting to punch in for the start of their shift. Without warning, Mack pulled out the handgun and shot the two men in front of him in the head, one of them after a brief chase. One died instantly. The other, miraculously, would recover. As stunned and frightened witnesses watched, Mack walked from the scene, weapon still in hand. He was not trying to escape. He was looking for a telephone from which to call his mother. By the time he found a telephone, helicopters were hovering over the scene and the sound of police sirens was moving closer.

Mack contacted his mother and, startlingly, gave her instructions for his funeral, including the music he wanted to be played. Among his choices were two songs from *Jesus Christ Superstar*, one of them, *I Don't Know How to Love Him*. He still had the .38-caliber handgun which, he said, he intended to use on himself. That had always been his intention, he said—his sole intention—to kill himself in a manner and in a place that would call media attention to what he perceived to be the callousness of corporate America. He had no intention of harming anyone else, he said, and had no recollection of having done so. Seventy-five minutes after he had belatedly arrived for his grievance hearing, Mack surrendered to authorities without further incident.

Mack was charged, arraigned, and brought to trial on several counts, including murder and attempted murder. His lawyer, a public defender, initially pleaded not guilty by reason of insanity on behalf of his client. Then he hinted that perhaps the plea would be changed, that the defense strategy would be to put corporate America on trial. His client, the lawyer said, was desperate and forlorn and in despair, a condition aggravated by the fact that he had been fired during the Christmas holiday season.

The first trial ended in a hung jury. The jurors were stymied, not on the question of guilt or innocence, but on the degree of guilt. Charges were refiled, a second trial was scheduled. Minutes before the second trial was to begin, the defense dropped another blockbuster. A plea bargain had been reached. Mack pleaded guilty to one count of murder, one count of attempted murder. Under terms of the plea bargain he would be sentenced to consecutive prison terms of life and 15 years to life.

Mack was asked by the judge whether he fully understood the terms of his plea, that he would not even be eligible for parole for at least 17 years. He understood, he said, then added, "I'm sorry the whole thing had to happen this way."

Had the second trial gone on, the prosecutor said later, there would have been some surprises. The prosecutor described Mack's testimony about a blackout and hallucinations—among them a huge orange blur and Mack's vision of himself riding a very large black cat—as "a bunch of hocus pocus." In a second trial, the prosecutor said, evidence would have been introduced about Mack's regular use of cocaine. The evidence was withheld in the first trial, the prosecutor said because, "I thought showing him as a guy with a clear mind going in there with a gun would have been more conducive to a first-degree conviction."

And then the prosecutor said: "Mr. Mack's good work record deteriorated in the last twelve months or so before he was fired, and I think this was brought on by his drug use. I think the drug use caused him to be late to work, to miss work, and to not have sufficient funds to carry on his lifestyle. I think his cocaine use was a factor in all that."

That such a glaring warning sign—a year of deteriorating performance after 24 years of good service—was overlooked is remarkable. That it might have been ignored is inexcusable. Yes, Robert Earl Mack unarguably fit the profile of the potentially dangerous employee.

"This is what you all get for firing me!"
Paul Calden, former employee, Fireman's Fund Insurance Co.

In January of 1993, a Tampa, Florida, man wearing a business suit shot at his former bosses in an office building cafeteria during lunchtime, killing three and wounding two. "This is what you all get for firing me!" he reportedly shouted. Paul Calden had been terminated eight months previously from Fireman's Fund Insurance Co.'s local office. He had visited a friend in the building several hours before the shooting and appeared calm then. When he returned shortly before 1 p.m., he went to the cafeteria, bought a soft drink and set it down on a table. Then he walked over to a group of people seated at a nearby table, pulled a gun from beneath his suit jacket and opened fire. All of the people shot were supervisors, managers, or executives. "It was not just a matter of him going into the cafeteria and just spraying in every direction," a police officer said. "He picked his targets."

A picture window behind where the victims were seated was shattered. Police had to calm cafeteria occupants, pick through broken glass, overturned tables, blood-stained carpets, and clothing. Initially, they thought Calden was still in the 12-story building after the shootings and made a room-by-room sweep, shouting for workers to stay in their offices. Later, the 33-year-old gunman was found dead from a self-inflicted gunshot wound to the head in a Clearwater park about 15 miles from the scene of the tragedy.

Could this violent scene have been avoided? The

executives of the company headquarters were so stunned they couldn't immediately confirm who had been killed and what had happened. Did this company have a policy concerning former employees' entering the building? Would it have been possible for a receptionist to notify security that he had entered? Perhaps not. While there is no foolproof method of anticipating violence, if the supervisor or receptionist understood the stresses that can affect a previously terminated employee, it is possible they might have forestalled the tragedy. The psychology of job loss is important. Companies should spend time training managers and workers to understand it.

"Everyone knew he had a short fuse."
Employee, U.S. Post Office - Royal Oak, MI

In the wake of the carnage at a regional postal center in Royal Oak, Michigan, on November 14, 1991, there were none of the customary expressions of surprise. Shock, yes, but not surprise.

For Thomas McIlvane, 31, who on that Thursday morning had invaded his former workplace armed with a sawed-off .22-caliber rifle and cold-bloodedly murdered three supervisors, there were no protestations that, "He always seemed like a nice guy." Or, "He was the last guy I would have expected to do anything like this." No testimonials about what a friendly neighbor, or good husband and father, he had been.

In the months preceding the horror in Royal Oak, in which he wounded six other persons before fatally shooting himself in the head, McIlvane had done just about everything short of running paid advertisements about his intentions. From the time he had been fired the previous year for "gross insubordination," the culmination of a long list of work-related offenses, McIlvane had repeatedly and publicly vowed revenge.

"Hey, everyone knew he had a short fuse," a fellow postal clerk said. "He told anyone who wanted to listen there'd be hell to pay if he wasn't reinstated. He even threatened some of the officials here over the telephone. The guy obviously had real problems."

McIlvane had, in fact, been brought to trial on a charge of making threats over the telephone. He had been acquitted. It was not the first time he'd come to the attention of the police. In May 1991, a permit that had been issued allowing McIlvane to carry a concealed weapon was revoked. During an investigation into complaints by McIlvane that he was being threatened, police became concerned that McIlvane might be "mentally unstable."

In light of McIlvane's employment record, reinstatement was unlikely. McIlvane, a martial arts enthusiast with a black belt in kick-boxing, had once been suspended for fighting with customers on his route. The suspension only fueled his rage, igniting what was to become a running dispute with postal managers.

"Yes, we were aware of his threats," a postal inspector said. "But this is a mail-processing facility. It is impossible to keep it locked up tight."

Six days prior to the massacre, McIlvane lost an arbitration hearing on a grievance filed on his behalf by his union. There was no other avenue of appeal. His dismissal was final. So was his chosen course of action.

WARNING SIGNS

Rarely in cases of violence in the workplace have warning signs been as evident as they were with McIlvane. In every case there is a warning sign, usually more than one, even though they're not exhibited as overtly and aggressively as in the case of McIlvane. The following list of warning signs is certain to be revised and expanded as case studies increase, but it is a good beginning, and represents reliable indicators of potential trouble.

1. Attendance Problems. Falling within this category are excessive sick leave, excessive tardiness, leaving work early, peculiar or improbable excuses for absences, higher absentee rate than other employees and on-the-job absenteeism (leaving the worksite without notice).

2. Impact On Supervisor/Manager's Time. Supervisors and managers have many responsibilities including staff development. However, if the supervisor is spending an inordinate amount of time coaching or counseling the individual concerning personal problems or having to redo the employee's work, it's a signal that the employee is in need of additional assistance outside the supervisor's expertise. The role of the supervisor is to develop skills and increase productivity, not to be a counselor. Make special note if, after repeated discussion, there is no change in the employee's performance.

3. Decreased Productivity. Be aware of any employee who has had a good-to-excellent performance record in the past but recently has been struggling at work or making excessive mistakes because of poor judgment or inattention. Note if he/she has missed project deadlines, assignments have been late, and wasting work time and materials. Any sudden change or pronounced deterioration in work performance should be recorded.

4. Inconsistent Work Patterns. The employee may be experiencing alternating periods of high and low productivity.

Often these extremes in the quality of work are due to substance abuse and/or alcohol abuse. Monitor the different degrees of productivity to see if there is a pattern.

5. Poor On-The-Job Relationships. Several signals may be given by this warning sign. Take note of any belligerent behavior, overreaction to criticism, mood swings and verbal harassment toward others.

6. Concentration Problems. A troubled employee is usually distracted and often has difficulty recalling job instructions, project details, and deadline requirements. You may see the troubled employee at his/her work station/office deep in thought of outside concerns. Often, he/she forgets badge, keys, wallet, or some other important items.

7. Safety Issues. Becoming more accident-prone is a clear indicator of stress. This individual is reckless concerning personal safety and will disregard safety guidelines for equipment, machinery, or vehicles. He/she will have a tendency to take needless risks without concern to other employees' safety.

8. Poor Health and Hygiene. Marked changes in personal grooming habits are important signals to note. The cessation of wearing makeup, no longer having hair done, clothes dirty or no longer pressed, or having the face unshaven when it was important to be nicely groomed in the past are all warning signs of internal conflict.

9. Unusual/Changed Behavior. This can include emotional outbursts, physical violence (i.e., hitting a wall or a piece of equipment), and/or unpredictable behavior. Inappropriate remarks, including vague or blatant threats. "Someone's going to pay." "This isn't right." "They'll get theirs," etc., are also signals. Others are statements which might be interpreted as delusional, such as referencing UFOs, the end of the world, being spied on, seeing elves, and secretive behavior.

10. Fascination with Guns or Other Weapons. Talks frequently about guns. Obsessed with the power of guns. Develops skills with different weapons. Likes to visit gun shops. Subscribes to gun magazines, like *Soldier of Fortune.*

11. Evidence of Possible Drug Use or Alcohol Abuse. The employee may act secretly around his/her locker, meet other employees or visitors in remote areas or take long lunches.

12. Evidence of Serious Stress in the Employee's Personal Life. Crying, excessive personal phone calls, bill collectors, recent separation, or death of a loved one.

13. Continual Excuses/Blame. Inability to accept responsibility for even the most inconsequential errors.

14. Unshakable Depression. Demonstrates depressed behavior for long periods of time (low energy, little enthusiasm expresses cynicism or despair).

Research into incidents of workplace violence discloses without exception the presence of at least several of these characteristics in the extremely enraged employee. On the day McIlvane returned for the last time to the postal center in Royal Oak, he qualified on several counts.

ALERT AND AVERT
In fairness to officials of the postal center, an alert of sorts had been sounded. A woman who worked on the loading

dock said afterward she had been told a month earlier by supervisors "to keep Tom McIlvane out if he showed up." Apparently she wasn't told how to accomplish that task.

On the morning of the murders neither she nor anyone else noticed McIlvane slip through an unlocked door used by employees, the sawed-off Ruger semiautomatic carbine apparently concealed beneath his clothing. He walked unwaveringly toward his prime targets, the supervisors, whipped out the rifle and began firing. Initially startled into immobility by the first sounds of gunfire, most of the more than 160 employees on duty quickly recovered and tried to barricade themselves in offices. Others tried to escape through exits, still others through windows. McIlvane walked away from the bodies, turned and began randomly spraying the area with gunfire. Six of his former co-workers were wounded. Then he turned the gun on himself. His murderous spree had taken six minutes. It had been months, perhaps years, in the making.

As a Royal Oak postal inspector said defensively, "It's impossible to keep it (in this case, a mail-processing facility) locked up tight." The unstated question is, what can be done? In this particular case, given what was known about McIlvane, a good security system would have been a valuable tool in averting workplace violence.

In addition to alerting and averting, there are even more valuable tools, and they're available to everyone at no cost. Eyes and ears. Don't just look, but see. Don't just listen, but hear. These steps can help you cope with disgruntled employees and perhaps head off tragedy.

NOTES

CHAPTER 5

"I GOTTA DO SOMETHING NOW, RIGHT NOW"

PATRICK HENRY SHERRILL

U.S. POST OFFICE - EDMOND, OKLAHOMA

The name probably means little today, but in 1986 it was seared into the public's consciousness. Probably more than any other single individual, Sherrill was responsible for making the general population keenly, painfully aware of a kind of terrorism that had been increasing annually but had for the most part been overlooked or ignored. He was soon to bring the issue of violence in the workplace into the media spotlight.

When Sherrill, 44, left work on August 19, 1986, he was furious. Only the intensity of his anger was different, not the anger itself. Sherrill, co-workers later recalled, was usually angry. Angry and surly. The gentlest thing that was said of him in retrospect was that he was often "solemn."

On that Tuesday, though, he was enraged. He had been reprimanded by his supervisor and told that he could expect a poor performance report. Although the possibility that he might lose his job had not been raised by the supervisor, who considered the meeting with Sherrill a counseling session, Sherrill obviously convinced himself that this would be the ultimate outcome, and that his 18 months with the postal service were about to come to an end.

Fuming with the perceived injustices rolling in his mind, Sherrill drove from the Edmond, Oklahoma, Post Office to the headquarters of the Oklahoma Air National Guard, where he was a weapons instructor. He was an expert marksman. He was also a former Marine and claimed he had served in Vietnam. According to his service record, however, he had never left the United States during his three-year hitch. Most of his tour of duty had been spent at Camp Lejeune, North Carolina. He was a communications and electronics technician and reached the rank of corporal.

According to some of the few people with whom Sherrill spoke regularly, it was not unusual for him to embellish his personal history. There was no doubt, however, that Sherrill was an expert marksman. He was a member of the Guard's marksmanship team and had been scheduled to compete later in the month in a national contest in Little Rock, Arkansas. The previous Saturday he had competed in a match near Edmond. For that competition he had checked out 200 rounds of ammunition. A day later he had been issued 300 additional rounds of ammunition, ostensibly to practice for the national competition.

Before leaving Guard headquarters that evening, Sherrill checked out two Colt .45-caliber pistols. A Guard spokesperson said Sherrill was allowed to check out weapons because he was a member of the marksmanship team. "We're very, very security conscious when it comes to issuing weapons," the spokesperson said.

Another spokesperson said, "There had been no reports, nothing medical, that would have precluded him from serving in the Guard or being a member of the marksmanship team. He was a quiet person, but he served the military well."

With his cache of weapons and ammunition, Sherrill returned to his home in Edmond. A police spokesman would later describe Sherrill's living quarters as "neat and orderly, but stacked up, almost to the ceiling in some places." Included in an inventory of the place were a homemade silencer, an old Japanese rifle, two BB air pistols, boxes with targets on them, targets on the walls, assumed to be mementos from shooting competitions, ham radios, a personal computer and hundreds of computer discs, all of them unlabeled. There were also video games, videotapes of the "World at War" television series, *Soldier of Fortune* magazines and copies of the English language *Soviet Life* magazine. Among Sherrill's books was a copy of *Russian Made Simple*. There was also a pamphlet that intrigued investigators for a time, *Dying: The Greatest Adventure of My Life—A Family Doctor Tells His Story.*

Ten sets of military fatigues, neatly folded, marksmanship medals, and a considerable amount of ammunition were found in another part of Sherrill's quarters. No note was found.

Whatever else Sherrill did on his last night, it's known he made two telephone calls to a postal union steward in Oklahoma City trying to arrange a transfer to the main post office. Sherrill had earlier complained to another union officer that his supervisors were picking on him and concluded with, "I gotta do something now, right now."

Early the next morning Sherrill donned his postal service uniform and packed his mail bag with two Colt .45-caliber pistols, a .22-caliber handgun and hundreds of rounds of ammunition. He then left for work, which was nearby, arriving shortly before 7:00 a.m. He entered the 20,000 square-foot work area in the rear of the post office through a back door and emerged with a weapon in each hand. Without speaking he walked up to two supervisors and shot them dead. (Ironically, the supervisor who had reprimanded Sherrill the day before was not present. He arrived late to work that day, arriving after the massacre had ended.) It was 7:05 a.m.

"I heard two quick shots and then a single shot," a survivor later recalled. "I thought it was a bunch of the guys clowning around, that maybe one of them had dropped a mail tray or something. But then I saw a guy fall with blood all over him. Then I heard another shot. And someone yelled, 'No! No!' Then another shot. And someone screamed, 'Oh, my God!'"

"He didn't have any preference about who he was shooting. Women and men, black and white. He shot anything that moved. People were scrambling everywhere, and he was shooting at everyone who was moving."

One witness dived behind a case where letters are sorted. He heard more shots and screams. He saw a fellow worker running down an aisle holding his side, blood oozing between his fingers. The terrified witness was desperately seeking an open door to escape. As he worked his way down the aisle, slowly and as quietly as possible, he glanced up an aisle.

"There were two people lying on the floor," he said. "Then I heard a supervisor yell, 'Get out of here, you crazy son of a bitch!' Then there were three more shots. He got her."

The last door on the witness's side of the building was open. He slipped through, then jumped on the hood of a passing car and told the startled driver to take him to the nearby police station. Others were less fortunate, including five women who huddled in terror in their three-sided work station, from which there was no escape route. Sherrill, unhurried, found them. He shot and killed four of them, wounded the other. He continued his prowl. He found four other employees huddled together. He shot and killed them all. One young worker rounded a corner carrying a bundle of papers. Sherrill shot him. His body was found still clutching the newspapers.

The workplace was now a din of screaming, weeping, and moaning, a place of unimaginable terror. Some of Sherrill's desperate prey tried to scramble to safety under tables. Sherrill coolly walked after them, then shot and killed them.

Outside the building a police SWAT team was trying to appraise the situation and trying to make contact with Sherrill by telephone and by bullhorn. The police had no way of knowing how many hostages Sherrill was holding, nor did they know how he would react if they were to attack. Their dilemma was compounded by the fact that most of the doors to the area were locked. Sherrill had perhaps locked some of them. Others were customarily chained shut by the postal service during night and early morning hours.

Finally, an open door was found, and an assault was mounted. But by that time Sherrill had claimed his last victim. He had placed one of his weapons against his head and pulled the trigger for the last time. His horrible toll: 14 dead, excluding himself, and six wounded. At that time, it was the third worst mass murder by a single gunman in the nation's history, surpassed only by the massacre at a McDonald's restaurant in San Ysidro, California, in 1984, in which 21 persons were killed, and the 16 persons killed in 1966 by a sniper from a tower at the University of Texas in Austin.

In one significant way, though, the slaughter in Edmond, Oklahoma, was perhaps the most horrifying of all. Sherrill was killing not strangers, but co-workers, people he knew at least by sight, some of whom he knew better than that. In the wake of the carnage one thing was clear: violence in the workplace was no longer an aberration. It was—is—a genuine menace that can strike at any time, in any place. It is a grave and major problem of contemporary society. And if it is not addressed, the repercussions are likely to be even more disastrous, the toll in personal tragedy even higher. And economically, it could be ruinous.

But the struggle against workplace violence is not hopeless; those who would fight it are not defenseless.

THE AFTERMATH

On a quiet, warm Sunday morning, the cremated remains of Patrick H. Sherrill were buried at the grave site of his parents in Watonga, Oklahoma. The private ceremony was attended by about 25 relatives and acquaintances. Among the relatives were a sister, who understandably still refused to talk with the media, a niece, and two nephews. One of the nephews read a brief eulogy, but at the family's request reporters were kept at a distance and were unable to hear what was said. The service lasted about two minutes. Five minutes after that, the area was deserted. Left behind was a bouquet from letter carriers in Irving, Texas. There was a card with the bouquet. It read: "To those who understand what he went through as a carrier. No one will ever know how far he was pushed to do what he did."

COLLECTIVE TRAUMA

On that same Sunday in Edmond, residents of the stricken town, still shocked and dazed and puzzled, were somberly walking into the football stadium at Central State

University for a memorial service. The governor of the state had declared that Sunday an official day of mourning, and almost 4,000 persons, including relatives of the victims, friends, co-workers, and survivors gathered for the 50-minute service. Hopefully, a minister said, the service would be the beginning of "our town's healing."

Attempts to heal had actually begun days earlier, within an hour or two of the tragedy, and in the vanguard as always were trained trauma response teams. Their job was not necessarily to mourn the dead, but to console the living, to ease their pain, to try to explain the seemingly inexplicable.

"There's no way of knowing with certainty what sort of psychological problems await the families of the dead and those who work in the Edmond Post Office, nor how long those problems will last," a psychologist said. "There's just so much hurt."

At the site of Sherrill's merciless, murderous rampage, a mail carrier said hoarsely, "Nothing will ever be normal here again. It's going to take some of us a long, long time to recover, if we ever do. A lot of innocence was wasted in there, and that won't go away overnight."

An industrial cleaning firm had worked long hours to try to erase reminders of the massacre inside the post office. The blood had been scrubbed away, but it was indelibly imprinted on the minds of many.

While trauma teams worked out of churches, schools, any available space, investigators continued to probe for information about Sherrill, interviewing anyone who knew him even just in passing.

Sherrill had been, they were quickly discovering, an enigmatic man. He was also, it was becoming increasingly clear, a disagreeable man. Typical of responses to their inquiries was this comment from a fellow worker at the Edmond Post Office: "He'd screw up and then make the same mistake again. And to hear him tell it, it was never his fault. He carried my route once. He didn't have any idea of what it meant to be a mailman. He was discourteous to people on the street. I had people mad at me the next day because he had carried the mail. They said he was very rude, and he misdelivered a lot of mail. Hell, he couldn't even find the Wal-Mart, and it's the biggest store in town."

FITTING THE PROFILE

With every opinion the investigators collected about Sherrill's character, one thing became increasingly obvious. Sherrill was, in many ways, the prototypical potentially violent employee. He had a tenuous grip on reality, among other symptoms. He was severely depressed. His history, particularly his fascination with guns and his abusive treatment of strangers, suggested a bent toward violence. According to co-workers, he was a continual blamer, refusing to accept responsibility for his own shortcomings. Only in the category of chemical dependence is the evidence less than overwhelming.

Sherrill also displayed several of the warning signs of an emotionally-enraged employee. His poor performance demanded a disproportionate share of his supervisors' time. His productivity continually decreased. His work patterns were inconsistent. He was often inefficient at his job. His relationships with fellow workers were, at best, strained. His concentration was scattered, as evidenced by his making the same mistakes over and over again. His bad temper and aggressiveness in dealing with the public were unmistakable signs of the unusual behavior that can precede a violent episode.

How, then, did such a potential menace escape detection? Why was he hired? Why wasn't he fired or, at the very least, urged to seek help? Sherrill's supervisors could not have been unaware of his problems in the workplace or with his co-workers. Part of the problem is that in the past the United States Postal Service apparently placed little credence in psychological profiles or "warning signs." That attitude doesn't make the Postal Service, which has the largest civilian work force in the country, unique. There has long been resistance toward acknowledging the importance and efficacy of the psychological profile in averting serious employee problems, including violence.

After the mass murders in the Royal Oak, Michigan, Post Office November 14, 1991, a postal service official admitted to having problems with a program designed to do a more effective job of screening potential employees.

"It's very difficult," he said. "It's relatively easy to find out what someone had done, but predicting what someone may do is nearly impossible."

He was wrong on both counts. The Postal Service customarily checks the military records of veterans, but those records, a postal official said, are sometimes very difficult to locate and retrieve. And, the same official said, obtaining employment information from private-sector employers can be even more difficult.

"Employers are very guarded about the type of information they're willing to share," the official said, "for fear that a negative comment could have legal ramifications later."

So discovering what a person has done is hardly cut and dried. Nor is predicting what a person may do "nearly impossible." In almost every case of murder in the workplace, the murderer fits into one or more of the categories from which an emotionally enraged employee is likely to come. More than that, the murderer almost unfailingly exhibited one or more of the warning signs of the emotionally enraged employee.

Psychological profiling admittedly is imperfect, as is any other science dealing with the unique minds of imperfect human beings, in all of their infinite variety. Occasionally a person will slip between the cracks, will not fit, will even defy the psychological profile.

Despite the specious arguments to the contrary, psychological profiling is effective and, coupled with the list of warning signs and other reliable indicators, is a major weapon in identifying, anticipating, and even defusing potential sources of workplace violence. A history of violence is still the most effective criterion for forecasting violent behavior. As is often the case, the major problem is not with the system, but with those who operate the system. The breakdown inevitably begins with that astute and now legendary observation of the redneck lawman in *Cool Hand Luke*, that "what we have here is a failure to communicate." In every case study of violence in the workplace, somewhere along the line, usually early on, there was a failure to communicate, often compounded by a failure to act, even when the warning signals burned as brightly as neon. From Larry Hansel to Patrick Sherrill, the signs were clearly there. And the same signs will be detected the next time headlines shriek about another incident of violence in the workplace. Once again it will be, tragically and needlessly, after the fact.

OVERSIGHTS
There are several factors to explain such oversights. Ignorance. Indifference. Misplaced loyalty. But a more common

(and human) factor is the desire, whether inbred or learned, to avoid confrontation. It's part and parcel of the ridiculous but comfortable, and still widely held, belief that if you ignore a problem, it will go away. From that comes the rationalization that, "Ah, Charlie's just having a bad day, but he'll be all right tomorrow, back to his old self. The last thing I want to do is make things worse for him by calling him on the carpet. The guy's got enough problems without that." With that view, Charlie's problems are almost certainly going to be your problems, perhaps with tragic consequences.

It's apparent that Patrick Sherrill's problems, among them his antisocial attitude and below average job performance, were generally ignored for a prolonged period at the Edmond Post Office, by supervisors, fellow workers, and union officials. When finally those problems could no longer be ignored, when they had to be addressed, the situation seems to have been handled clumsily. The result was appalling.

Just as surely there could have been no mistaking the depth of Thomas McIlvane's rage long before he embarked on his murderous rampage in Royal Oak, Michigan. Well before the act McIlvane had, in effect, threatened, within earshot of many, to kill one of his supervisors. In case after case of workplace violence there is similar evidence of forewarning. The signs were there. The signs are usually there, although perhaps not always as obvious as with Sherrill and McIlvane.

REPORT THREATENING SITUATIONS
In the wake of the Royal Oak murders, the U.S. Postal Service was deluged with telephone calls to a hot line that had been used primarily to report allegations of fraud. The new floods of calls were, for the most part, reports of threatening situations at work. More than 300 of the calls were serious enough to warrant investigation. Seven arrests were made for

threats against supervisors and co-workers. The reaction on the hot line was a culmination of six years during which 36 persons were killed by current or former postal workers in a series of incidents.

Fear undoubtedly was a factor in the hot line response, but so, too, was the promise of anonymity. But whatever the motivation, a line of communication had been opened, the indispensable first step toward averting disaster. Perhaps it's not the ideal system, but it's at least a start. There's no way of knowing if one of those eight arrests prevented a later tragedy.

Back in 1992 when we were working on the first edition of this book, the hot line was the extent of the progress the Postal Service had made in devising a policy to cope with workplace violence. There was broad agreement that the workplace and the nature of the work were a significant part of the problem for the Postal Service, as is what a former postmaster called the agency's intransigent "corporate culture." Among supervisors, he said, it's expressed in an attitude toward subordinates of, "I paid my dues, now it's your turn."

At that time the Postal Service and the four postal unions had frequently discussed the issue of violence in the workplace, but their relationship was so adversarial they had been unable to draft a policy statement. The largest of the unions suspected that such a joint statement would be used by the Postal Service as a public relations ploy. The union preferred an independent study of the workplace to identify problems. Another "failure to communicate." One step forward, two steps back. And the next tragedy awaits.

Today the United States Postal Service has provided its employees and managers with a comprehensive, state-of-the-art workplace violence prevention training program. It appears that the training and immediate intervention programs are working. Our organization has had the privilege of training more than 75,000 Postal employees over the last few years and providing advanced Threat Assessment Team training to their leadership and clinical teams.

THE EFFECTS OF POST-TRAUMATIC STRESS

The husky, bearded man sobbed convulsively. After agonizing minutes he lifted his face from his large hands and smiled almost sheepishly, as if embarrassed.

"Sorry," he said softly. "Sometimes it just happens, you know? Something brings back a memory, and there I go. Like, you know what I was just thinking about? That the Sooners are playing in Norman this Saturday. Homecoming. And we won't be there. He won't be there ever again. I doubt I will, either. We had season tickets for years, never missed a home game."

He looked down and said again, "Sorry."

Almost two months had passed since Patrick H. Sherrill had walked into the post office and murdered 14 fellow employees and wounded six others before fatally shooting himself in the head. Sherrill's toll of casualties was actually much greater than that. The sobbing man, for instance, was also one of Sherrill's victims even though he'd suffered no physical injury. He had suffered grievous loss. He'd suffered severe emotional and psychological pain, which would take an indeterminate time to heal, if ever.

The man had lost his best friend, who was shot dead without warning, where he stood by Sherrill, the man with whom he had shared so many happy Saturday afternoons at University of Oklahoma football games. Like countless others who had been in the post office that fateful morning, in addition to families and friends of the slain 14 victims, the sobbing man had been undergoing counseling and therapy, which had started only hours after the tragedy. As the scope of the tragedy became known, the people of Edmond and all of Oklahoma had commandeered churches, schools, any available space to set up trauma centers. Not long after those initial steps had been taken, skilled, highly trained trauma response units from all over the country were descending on Edmond. Sherrill's murderous rampage was over; the work of the trauma response teams was just beginning. And it would go on indefinitely, perhaps for a lifetime in many cases.

How to console the inconsolable? How to make even a semblance of sense out of the senseless? What to tell a family suddenly deprived of a husband and father who had gone in to work on his day off because the office was short-handed? What words of consolation are there for a man who shortly before had moved his family from Atlanta to Edmond to accept a promotion in the postal service and who had, only a few days before the shootings, shared his wife's excitement over her hiring as a part-time clerk in the Edmond post office? She had been one of Sherrill's last victims—at the start of her fourth day on the job.

"We'll go back to work," one of the survivors said, "because we have to go back to work, don't we? But I don't know how long it takes to get over something like this, or if you ever get over it. For some of us it's probably going to take a lot longer than others. But however long it takes, things will never be the same around here again. Never. Too much grief. Too much pain. Too many memories. And I don't want anyone telling me that after awhile things will get back to normal. It won't happen. Not here. Not ever."

Time, though, is indeed the great healer, and the healing

process can be helped immeasurably by trained trauma teams, as was the case in Edmond. Indeed, many corporations, finally acknowledging that violence in the workplace is undeniably increasing, have taken steps that would, optimally, avert disaster or, failing that, ease the transition from trauma to healing and back to productivity. Key to such a transition is the interaction between Human Resources professionals, victim service providers, senior management, and the psychological trauma team assisting the company in rebuilding the vision and goals of the organization.

COSTS TO ORGANIZATIONS AND EMPLOYEES

When violence in the workplace occurs, the cost in human terms extends far beyond the immediate loss of life. In addition to the human suffering, the company itself will suffer many costs:

- Security
- Building repair and cleanup
- Business interruptions with customers
- Loss of productivity
- Lost work time
- Turnover of employees
- Salary continuation for those who are injured or traumatized
- Valued employees quitting or retiring early
- Increase in workers' compensation claims
- Increase in medical claims
- Increase in insurance premium rates
- Costs of attorney fees, medical care, and psychological care for current employees.

For example, the costs to the Elgar Corporation were estimated at $400,000 in addition to those covered by insurance, and an estimated premium increase of $100,000 yearly for workers' compensation. The estimated cost to General Dynamics amounted to $1.2 million in addition to expenses covered by insurance.

There are sound business reasons for companies to provide prompt trauma therapy after a violent incident in the workplace. According to statistics from Crisis Management International in a November 1991, study made by the Barrington Psychiatric Center in Los Angeles, of 200 people suffering major psychic trauma, the half that were treated soon after the incident averaged 12 weeks' recovery time before returning to work and only 13 percent chose litigation. Of the other half of the group, not treated immediately, they required 46 weeks for recovery time and 94 percent chose litigation.

NOTES

PART II

UNDERSTANDING
HUMAN BEHAVIOR

CHAPTER 6

BASIC HUMAN NEEDS

THE MEANING OF WORK

Related to the ability to assist employees with the stresses in their lives, there is the need for a greater understanding of the value and meaning that work has for all of us. Unsurprisingly, it was Sigmund Freud who developed the first comprehensive theory about personality. The renowned psychiatrist contended that there were two primary sources of happiness and contentment in life. He identified them as:

1. The need for love. Everyone needs to have an intimate relationship with another person, or with a family unit. Without it, our feelings of significance in the world are greatly diminished.

2. The need for work. Everyone also needs to have purposeful activity that identifies his/her role in, and his/her contribution to, society.

Abraham H. Maslow, regarded as the father of humanistic psychology, is famous for his "hierarchy of human needs." He argued that human motives can be placed in an hierarchy of prominence. That is, some needs demand satisfaction before others. Maslow placed these needs in five hierarchical levels. (See Chart A.) Although there are exceptions, typically we satisfy the needs at the lower levels before becoming concerned with the needs at the higher levels.

Chart A

HIERARCHY OF HUMAN NEEDS

.

SELF ACTUALIZATION NEEDS

ESTEEM NEEDS
Admiration & Respect
Perceive self as competent & achieving

BELONGINGNESS & LOVE NEEDS

Friendship & Love

SAFETY NEEDS

Security, Stability, Structure, Protection

PHYSIOLOGICAL NEEDS

Air, Thirst, Hunger, Sleep

Food, as a physiological need, is the most basic level of

need. Water, air, and sleep are also among the most demanding physiological needs, which must be satisfied before moving on to other levels.

For example, if a person is hungry, his/her behavior will center on obtaining food. Until this need is met, that person will not be concerned about making new friends or developing a career. Most of us progress up the hierarchy over the course of a lifetime based on our perceptions of our relative safety, security, and belongingness in our changing life circumstances.

OTHER LEVELS OF HUMAN NEEDS:

1. Safety Needs. When physiological needs are met, we become increasingly motivated by our safety needs. These include the need for security, stability, protection, freedom from fear or chaos, and the need for structure and order. These needs may become dominant where the future is murky or when the stability of the political, social or work order is threatened. Current concern over the economy has led many to refrain from buying, to delay starting or adding to a family, or to take less risks at work. When people perceive a threat to their security, they will react by trying to build savings accounts, or by seeking out a job with greater security and minimal risk. They may seek out the orderliness of the military, or organized religion. People with strong safety or security needs may tend to stay in an unhappy work relationship or in an unhappy marriage.

2. Belongingness and Love Needs. For most of us, the need for food and water and the need for safety and stability are fairly well satisfied. It's only when our financial resources are threatened that we become concerned about our physiological and safety needs. But satisfaction of these lower-level needs does not end our quest for happiness. The need for friendship and love soon emerges. Most of us find that an exclusive devotion to producing income is unsatisfying if it means sacrificing time spent with friends and loved ones.

3. Esteem Needs. Regardless of centuries of wistful poetry to the contrary, there is more to life than love, Maslow contends. Satisfaction of our belongingness and love needs will invariably direct our attention to our esteem needs. The perception of oneself as competent and achieving and the presence of respect from others are the foundations of self-esteem. Satisfying such needs is not self-serving narcissism. Failure to do so can result in feelings of inferiority, helplessness, and discouragement.

4. The Need for Self-actualization. Nearly every culture has a myth about a protagonist/hero who, by virtue of a magic lamp or contact with a supernatural being, receives everything he or she wishes. Health, wealth, love, and power. Imagine their surprise when they discover, as they inevitably do, that everything isn't enough, at least not enough to produce total happiness. Instead there's a strange new discontent and restlessness. Something's missing. That something is self-fulfillment. And so begins (for those who have satisfied their needs at the base of the pyramid), a personal quest to develop themselves to their full potential. They introspectively and repeatedly ask what they want out of life, where their lives are headed, what they want to accomplish. Many never have the opportunity to explore these questions as they become absorbed in the day-to-day fight to pay their bills and feed their families.

What Freud and Maslow have in common and with other psychologists and psychiatrists is a recognition of the value and meaning of work whether that work is perceived by the individual as a career or "just a job." In an emotionally charged and volatile time where competition for jobs is stiff, it's imperative that employers be aware of that value and meaning to their employees, particularly if they are taking it away.

Many companies, aware of the seriousness of the situation, will have trained personnel, as well as trauma counselors, available onsite when a layoff is announced. The burgeoning outplacement industry in recent years is an indication of growing sensitivity to the impact which the loss of a job can have on an individual. It is not possible to measure how many potentially violent employees were averted from taking retaliatory measures because of this conscious intervention.

STRUGGLE FOR ESTEEM
Alfred Adler believed that as weak and helpless children we are surrounded by and dependent for survival upon larger and stronger adults. The counterpoint to dependence is independence, a yearning intensified by the passage of time. First comes a desire for equality, eventually supplanted by what Adler called "humankind's need to strive for superiority."

Striving for superiority, Adler contended, was the motivating force in life. Virtually everything we do, he said, is designed to establish a sense of superiority over life's obstacles, to overcome feelings of inferiority. And the more inferior we see ourselves, the stronger our striving for superiority.

This innate need to strive for superiority has impact on all facets of life, including work. Adler parallels Freud in believing that work is one of only three indispensable life tasks at which every human being desires to achieve superiority. The others are the need for friends and the need to love and be loved. (See Chart B.)

Chart B

ONE OF THREE LIFE TASKS

.

WORK

Value & Meaning
Of Life & Work Today

FRIENDS   LOVE

Studies show that work, friends, and love affect one another and are, in fact, practically symbiotically linked. For example, if we are unhappy in our job, that experience will affect our relationship with our family and our friends. A bad day at work is almost unfailingly a harbinger of a bad night at home. It's a safe bet that even Ward Cleaver of the TV program, "Leave It To Beaver," occasionally stewed sullenly over a setback at work and was grumpy with June and the boys.

Conversely, if we are unhappy at home it will have an impact on our productivity and satisfaction at work. Personal problems, whatever they are—financial, family, marital, health—cannot be conveniently stashed in a briefcase and deposited at the door of the workplace, to be picked up at the end of the day. John Taylor is an example of this principle.

STRESS INDEX

The third leg of the equilateral triangle of life's tasks is work, which has value infinitely beyond that of being a mere source of income. In contemporary society work is (perhaps unfortunately) how a person is defined. You meet a stranger at a party or at some other social gathering. After the mandatory, "How are you?" the next question is almost guaranteed to be, "What do you do?" Even more important, work is a primary source of friendships.

For many, work is a source of structure and order. It implies routine and stability in a chaotic and uncertain world. These factors compound the pain when there is a significant change, such as a termination or a layoff. The inborn sense of feeling inferior described by Adler becomes magnified, intensified, and in some cases unbearably so. To compensate for the heightened feeling of inferiority, the need to strive for superiority also becomes greater. For some the fastest and most accessible way to gain or regain a feeling of superiority is with a gun. So it was for Larry Hansel. So it was for John Taylor. And the list keeps growing. And each new tragedy forces, or should force, a painful new re-examination of the value and meaning of work. And, hopefully, a more enlightened examination.

UNDERSTANDING LOSS

Other factors should be considered when contemplating the value and meaning of work to an individual. An employee does not necessarily need to be terminated to suffer substantial loss. Loss of stature, income or opportunities, such as with a job change or a demotion can be as devastating and provocative. The perception of, or actual loss of, any of the following may be a catalyst for retaliation:

1. Job Satisfaction. Some define job satisfaction as doing what you want to do. The bonus is that you get paid for it too! A job that allows you to use your motivated skills and abilities in work that contributes to or enhances your ideals is satisfying. A job that allows you to maximize your capabilities is satisfying. Being transferred to a job with equal pay but tedious, unfulfilling work undercuts self-esteem and job satisfaction.

2. Growth Opportunities. Many place great value and importance on having room to grow personally and/or professionally. This doesn't necessarily mean zooming up the corporate ladder. What it does mean is that the job tasks are new learning experiences that stimulate growth.

3. Monetary Rewards. Many judge themselves and others by the money they earn. For them, success as a person is measured in dollars. They feel diminished even if their income goes from $400,000 to $300,000. One angry senior executive complained, "They might as well have cut my balls off," when his salary was trimmed from $350,000 to $325,000. Clearly, he had ample to live on. At issue for him was his self-esteem. His image of himself was of someone who moved steadily upward in income and position, without setback. Whether compensation is satisfactory to an individual is determined not only by economic need, but frequently also by what money represents to an individual. This is not a trivial consideration when compensation reductions are planned.

SELF-ESTEEM
Many employees, driven by that innate drive for

superiority, may perceive a threat to their self-esteem with the loss of any of the above. When that realization sets in, productivity and efficiency levels go down. The levels of anger and resentment go up. A dead-ended employee, an employee stripped of hope for advancement or betterment, is a potentially stressed employee and, given the presence of other stressors, a potentially emotionally enraged employee.

IDENTIFYING THE SIGNALS

There are some straightforward signals which help to identify an employee who is struggling with the results of stress:

1. Disorganized Behavior. Organization and planning skills begin to suffer. The employee begins to forget where he or she placed items, begins to forget important details.

2. Heightened Anxiety. Manifestations of elevated anxiety include increased body aches or headaches, changes in sleep, eating or sex patterns, changes in blood pressure, and muscle tension.

3. Personality Magnification. A fast-paced, task-oriented individual with a tendency to be aggressive and assertive becomes even more pushy and demanding An individual with a tendency to avoid problems will continue to do so to avoid confrontation, even as resentment grows.

4. Defensive Posture. Suggestions once graciously accepted are now interpreted as browbeating. There are complaints of being "constantly used" and "picked on." Defense mechanisms often operate on a subconscious level. Thus, one may not be immediately aware of the reasons he/she is acting in particular ways.

HOW MANAGERS AND
SUPERVISORS CAN HELP

What does all of this mean to the supervisor who is genuinely concerned about the welfare of his/her employees? Or to the Human Resources manager concerned about the company's overall health and vitality as well as profitability, who is anxious to provide sound coaching to supervisors on employee relations matters?

UNDERSTANDING THE PSYCHOLOGY OF LOSS

First, it means **understanding the psychology of job loss.** This means that any necessary "take-aways," or events that run the risk of appearing to be take-aways, should be orchestrated and planned with the same forethought and care as a major relocation, merger, or product launch. These "take-aways" include compensation, benefits, bonuses, title, perks, special privileges, communication, vehicles, freedoms, space, opportunities, or keys. It means understanding that "loss" can include those things both material and intangible. It means understanding that, when the environment is uncertain and resources are diminished, people will hang on that much tighter to what they have, and will be that much more threatened by the potential loss of that which they value. It means **noticing** what has value to different employees under one's supervision, and knowing that what they value will differ from employee to employee.

OBSERVATION

Secondly, it means **becoming careful observers of human behavior** and becoming alert to changes in behavior—not only in the more vocal employees, but in those less expressive as well.

INTERVENTION

Third, it means **intervening to assist the employee** who is exhibiting signs of being overly stressed. This assistance may not be direct. A well-timed management referral of an employee to the company's Employee Assistance Program (EAP) is frequently the most wise, practical, and efficient measure a supervisor or Human Resources manager can take. The EAP provides assessment, counseling, and referral by trained professionals, while the supervisor provides performance coaching, encouragement, support, and resolution of work-related problems and obstacles. The supervisor **cannot** control the behavior of an employee, but he or she does exert profound influence on the employee's immediate environment, and therefore on the employee's daily job experiences.

Clearly, not every employee who snaps at co-workers, misplaces items, expresses extreme religious or political views, or is fearful of losing his or her job is a potentially violent employee. The key point is, that in every instance of workplace violence, the emotionally enraged employee had experienced a build-up of life stresses over time. There came a point for each of them when it became simply too much to bear. The vigilant supervisor (or co-worker or family member) who moves promptly to assist the employee in alleviating those stresses, may very well save lives (even his/her own life).

RESPONSIBLITY

Does this mean that supervisors of emotionally enraged employees are to blame for their employees' actions? Absolutely not. The life/work situations leading to violent behavior are complex. Human Resource specialists do not have 100 percent accurate means for predicting and preventing violence in all cases. We are all responsible, however, for educating ourselves and others to become better observers of behavior and to increase the chances of averting crises before they happen.

Unfortunately, there is no foolproof system for detecting emotionally enraged employees, but there are guidelines, and there are warning signs. Some are subtle, some are as bright as a flare. Understanding these signs, recognizing them when they occur—and acting on that knowledge and recognition—are vital steps in heading off possible tragedy.

NOTES

CHAPTER 7

"I told them I'd be back."
PROFILE OF A PERPETRATOR

THE STANDARD GRAVURE CORPORATION

On September 14, 1989, Wesbecker, 47, arrived unexpectedly at the Standard Gravure Corporation, a three-story printing plant in Louisville, Kentucky. His appearance was unexpected because for the past 13 months Wesbecker, a pressman, had been on disability for emotional problems.

Wesbecker parked his red Chevrolet Monza near a door of the building, reached inside the car and pulled out a brown and blue leather duffel bag. As he advanced unchallenged and unimpeded toward the building, Wesbecker literally bumped into a departing co-worker at the entrance.

"I said, 'How are you, Rock?' (Wesbecker's nickname) and he said, 'Fine, John. Back off and get out of the way. Back off. All the way to the wall.'"

And then Wesbecker said, "I told them I'd be back. Get out of my way, John. I told them I'd be back."

Wesbecker walked to the elevator, stepped in and punched the button for the third floor, the executive offices. The door slid open. Wesbecker stepped out and, without a word, shot a receptionist. Without pause, he turned and shot another employee. The massacre had begun. Before it was over, Wesbecker killed seven persons and wounded 15 others. His last shot was into his own head.

Police later recovered the duffel bag. In it they found two semiautomatic 9-millimeter handguns, a .38-caliber revolver, a bayonet, more than 20 boxes of ammunition and numerous clips for an AK-47 assault rifle. Police couldn't determine whether the AK-47, the weapon used by Wesbecker during his bloody escapade, and the handgun he later used to kill himself had been carried in the duffel bag or had been carried by hand.

After the first shootings, Wesbecker followed a walkway from the Standard Gravure building to the **Courier Journal** newspaper building, then walked down the stairs to the basement. He shot one person in the stairwell. Upon reaching the basement, he shot another. He then walked up to the first floor and began firing randomly with the assault rifle. Said one official, "It appears he was just shooting whoever happened to come in range of the automatic weapon."

In the aftermath it became evident that Wesbecker's murderous fury had not only been predictable, it had almost become inevitable. Wesbecker had worked for Standard Gravure, which prints inserts and Sunday supplements for newspapers nationwide, for 20 years, and for most of that time was, according to a co-worker, "one of the nicest guys you'd ever work with, up until the time he began to have emotional problems. He had difficulty with the company as he perceived them."

Another acquaintance of Wesbecker's traced the first noticeable changes to Wesbecker's divorce a few years earlier. Still another acquaintance said he'd become concerned two years earlier when Wesbecker became an avid reader of *Soldier of Fortune* magazine and began to mention ordering a Uzi, an Israeli semiautomatic weapon.

Then it was reported that before Wesbecker had been placed on disability at about 60 percent of his annual income, he had asked for a less stressful job and had a doctor's recommendation to back his request. The company ignored the recommendation and rejected the request.

"That's when his mental problems really began," a co-worker said.

This was one of Wesbecker's major clashes with management at Standard Gravure, a company allegedly beset with morale problems, but hardly the only one. He complained often—to his union, to co-workers—about what he perceived to be unfair treatment.

"He was very bitter with the owner and the chief executive of the company, and some of the supervision in the pressroom itself," a union official said. "He wanted to work at a less stressful job, which they couldn't work out, or he wanted to retire at a better level than what they actually gave him. And then he began to worry that his disability benefits were going to run out."

A co-worker said, "You didn't have to be a genius to figure out something bad was going to happen. We're talking about a guy who was being treated as a manic depressive, a guy who had tried to commit suicide three times, a guy who was becoming more paranoid by the day. When he was put on disability he made some threats, not veiled threats, that he'd get even with them. He was talking about it for a year."

Company officials said they had no prior knowledge of any threats. With or without overt threats, it seems in retrospect that there were enough warning signs for someone in authority in the company to have been alerted to the possibility of the presence of an emotionally enraged employee. A terrible tragedy might have been averted.

There is a footnote to this tragedy, as there invariably is. As police searched the area after the massacre, an officer discovered a man huddled in a corner, shuddering uncontrollably. "He hadn't been shot or wounded physically," the officer said. "He was just in shock, terrified and horrified."

He was one of many unregistered victims of workplace violence, those who don't show up on death tolls or lists of the physically wounded. He is one of the traumatized, requiring perhaps years of counseling, destined to recall vividly in a recurring nightmare what one police veteran called a "battle zone, the worst I've seen since I was in Nam. A lot of carnage. So much blood. So many people."

THE PROFILE

The typical person likely to commit murder in the workplace is likely to give off warning signs that, unfortunately, go unheeded by those who work with the individual. Tom Harpley of National Trauma Services says, "The workplace murderer is likely to be a middle-aged Caucasian male, using an exotic weapon, such as an Uzi, an AK-47 or a Samurai sword, legally acquired. He usually has a fascination with such weapons."

There is a demographic and psychological profile of a violent employee, and although generalization is risky and perhaps even suspect, to some the profile of an emotionally enraged employee has proven uncommonly consistent.

Such a person is generally a male:

- Is 25 to 40 years of age
- Has a history of violence
- Is a loner
- Owns several guns
- Has, in the past, requested some type of assistance
- Is an angry person with little outlet for that anger
- Has a history of interpersonal conflict
- Is often socially withdrawn and most likely has family/ marital problems
- Will, after a while, stop expressing himself verbally and become introverted, whereas earlier he constantly verbalized his complaints to management and about management
- Becomes paranoid about others
- Exhibits self-destructive behavior, such as taking drugs or excessive drinking.

Almost without exception, the employee who has exploded into murderous rage has fit some facet of this profile, even the "model employee" John Taylor. Usually more than one facet of the profile applies, such as with Larry Hansel, sometimes all of the above facets, such as in the case of Joseph T. Wesbecker.

NOTES

PART III

PREVENTION AND MANAGEMENT PLANNING

NOTES

CHAPTER 8

SECURITY AND PREVENTION

WHY PLANS AND PROGRAMS
ARE NEEDED

HUMAN AND ECONOMIC COSTS

As previously mentioned, when violence occurs in the workplace, the cost in human terms extends far beyond the immediate loss of life. In addition to the human suffering of personnel and their families, the company itself will suffer many costs: increased security expenses, building repair and cleanup, business interruptions, productivity loss, lost work time, turnover of employees, salary continuation for those who are injured or traumatized, workers' compensation, medical claim increases and premium rate increases, attorney fees, medical costs, and psychological care for current employees. Plans can prevent human suffering and save a lot of money.

For employees the ramifications of losing a job are pervasive and cut deeply. The loss of a job (or of things of value in the work situation) is perceived as an assault to one's dignity and self-esteem. A person's security, stability and structure is jeopardized.

These are times when materialism erodes traditional values. It's an economy that has been described as techno-Darwinian, which means the weapons have changed but only the fittest still survive. And the fittest apparently are those companies that adhere to the five contemporary commandments of business:

- Make money
- Save money
- Increase production
- Cut costs
- Solve problems

The bitter reality is that cutting costs today is almost automatically equated with down-sizing, and often with massive layoffs. And the ranks of the jobless—for the most part, the embittered jobless—swell.

Another reality is that solving problems rarely applies to the personal problems of the worker, who too often is considered a replaceable part. A favored argument is that no supervisor, whether responsible for a dozen workers or several dozen, has either the time or the qualifications to deal with the personal problems of his/her subordinates. The supervisor may not be able to solve the personal problem, but he or she is the first line of defense for getting the solution started. The supervisor is at least aware that such problems exist. And he/she should also be aware of what help is available to try to cope with such problems. It's infinitely better and easier to deal with a small problem before it becomes a big problem, possibly a tragic problem.

The cost of not having a crisis management plan to cope with unforeseen events such as the Exxon Valdez tragedy or the Bophal disaster in India, can be high. Businesses can lessen the total impact of violent incidents by having management plans in place.

SECURITY DEVELOPMENT

One of the first steps for your company to take to prevent violence or to cope with its aftermath is a survey of your security arrangements and of current services available.

1. Define the company assets that need protection. An analysis should be done to determine what the organization needs to protect. Through the help of the security director (if you have one), facility engineer, facility operations manager, law enforcement agencies or a security agency, a thorough analysis of your facility should be undertaken.

You may not be able to afford all the recommendations from the professionals. However, a prioritized list will be helpful, so that you may do what is reasonable financially and culturally.

For example, installing a silent alarm button at the receptionist's desk that will immediately notify security, management, and police is cost-effective and smart. Another is to move the receptionist behind a glass partition and locked door.

Double doors with a security guard at the entrance of a building, where one cannot enter without a proper access badge may be more costly, but provide greater security.

2. Establish priorities for providing protection. Since senior management, Human Resources professionals, and supervisors are primary targets in workplace violence incidents, determine the best location in the facilities that would provide best protection and a secondary exit leading away from the facility. Receptionists are often the first to encounter an angry person and subject to attack. They do need protection and should be given a high priority.

3. Assess the organization's capability in responding quickly to workplace violence. In order to respond effectively to a violent incident, a crisis management team must be in place. Team members should be selected in advance from departments such as Human Resources, Legal, Security, and Facility Management. Telephone numbers of the team members should be in the rolodex of every manager. Along with the police number, the crisis management team phone number should be on the phone for speed dialing so everyone can respond immediately.

4. Establish written policies so there is clear communication between employees and management concerning veiled threats. Supervisors should be aware of their chain of command concerning potential violence of employees, and should not be viewed as hysterical or over-reacting if they mention concern about any particular employee. Corporate guidelines should be developed concerning proper responses to threats, employee harassments, warning potential victims, and notifying police. Consult labor attorneys and psychological professionals so that guidelines are legally and behaviorally sound. Make sure the written policies are followed to avoid unnecessary litigation.

5. Provide training programs and tools for pre-employment screening and for identification of potential behavioral problems. Interview training, checking of references, and low-cost assessment tools can save the company unnecessary pain concerning unstable employees. Awareness training should be provided as part of the indoctrination process as well as continued in-service training. Part of supervisory training should be to keep the team aware of the warning signs of erratic behavior.

6. Make policies concerning termination.
Termination training is a must for every organization and is best handled through the Human Resources department. Often, improper methods are utilized by supervisors and managers in terminating an employee. A constant theme from angry former employees is not that they were terminated, but how they were terminated. Many could not leave with their dignity intact. Consult with an outplacement firm on proper termination procedures.

For a potentially dangerous former employee, appropriate locks should be changed. Badges, parking passes, and any company property must be returned at the time of termination. Consider adding security personnel. Security guards can be uniformed or not, depending at what awareness level you wish your employees to have. Encourage co-workers that know the former employee to keep management advised if additional threats are made. Make note of the make and license number of former employees' automobiles.

7. Establish psychiatric resources or outplacement counseling to assist former employee. This can provide a valuable service to the organization and to the disgruntled employee. Although confidentiality is essential in a therapeutic relationship, certain states have laws requiring that clinicians warn a person in danger concerning potential violence. Outplacement consultants are not under the same constraints, so their observation of the former employee during job transition can help determine for you his or her mental outlook and likelihood of potential danger.

Once a crisis management plan has been developed, organizations should keep copies in more than one place. Many companies have disaster plans that cover natural disasters such as earthquakes and fire which they should be able to modify to cover other kinds of violence.

DEVELOPING A MANAGEMENT PLAN

Each company needs to assess its own situation and develop policies to address a violent situation. The form the plan takes can be detailed and comprehensive, or more simple and direct. There is a need to study what has happened in the past and what can be learned from past experiences. Besides **Prediction and Prevention Plans,** companies also need to develop a **Trauma Plan** as part of the positive management of violence at work. This will be discussed in a later chapter. Prediction of possible violent acts is one of the first steps to take.

PREDICTION — TYPES OF VIOLENCE

Violent incidents occur in three situations. First, when an employee is angry with management; second, when a customer or outside client is angry with a provider or denier of a product or service; and third, when an outside violent person by chance attacks a place of business or takes hostages. An example is the case of Lexus Corporation in Torrance, California, when an outsider, who had no previous contact with the company or its products, broke in and took hostages at rifle point because he was upset over his inability to find a job. The Elgar Corporation tragedy involved an employee, and the Quintessence Co. involved a contract janitorial worker.

Due to the increase in interpersonal violence, something needs to be done to predict the likelihood of violent behavior. J. Mercy and P. O'Carroll, authors of *Violence And Victims* recommend a public health approach that focuses on prevention rather than on the treatment of injury after violence has occurred. Other specialists believe that we can and should predict violence, yet acknowledge that whether predictions are made subjectively or statistically, they reflect inaccuracies. However, even though totally accurate prediction is impossible except in extreme circumstances, employers should not ignore the potential for workplace violence. In fact, employers may be held legally accountable for not predicting potential violence.

Some employees will send warnings in much the same way suicidal persons may try to alert others as to their intentions. Employees contemplating violence may be troubled and disturbed by their thoughts and hope someone will intervene. While the ability to predict violence is controversial, guidelines can be established to assist management in identifying potential problems.

PREVENTION PLAN—WORKING WITH POTENTIALLY VIOLENT EMPLOYEES

James S. Cawood, author of "On the Edge: Assessing the Violent Employee" in **Security Management**, 1991, recommends taking the following actions:

STEP 1 - Develop a written plan for handling threats. It should specify that reports be made to Human Resources, not a manager or supervisor, because co-workers may be reluctant to report to their immediate supervisor.

STEP 2 - Make an immediate investigation by interviewing the person who reports the threat as well as any other witnesses to the incident. Gather as much information as possible about the threat and the person making it. Document this information in detail.

STEP 3 - Contact a specialist in assessing potentially violent employees to review the information and decide if further action is necessary.

STEP 4 - If an additional investigation is warranted, form a crisis management team, which includes Legal Counsel, Human Resources, and Security.

STEP 5 - Together with the specialist, develop a plan with this team. This can include a background investigation of the employee. Emphasis should be directed to locating information indicative of how the employee responds to stress and should consider the predictors of violence outlined in Chapter 2. Past military service or interest in weapons should be included. The investigation must be handled discreetly to shield the company from later claims of libel, slander, or invasion of privacy.

STEP 6 - The specialist should interview the person who reported the threat and any others who can verify or provide additional information on the employee's state of mind. This must be done discreetly so as not to alert the suspected employee.

STEP 7 - The employee should be interviewed directly by the specialist. Provide security if it is believed the employee will become enraged. Security should be experienced and trained to handle the situation. Calm, low-key, security individuals who do not project a threatening or officious manner are recommended. Their behavior should not precipitate an incident of violence.

STEP 8 - Give the employee the rest of the day off after the interview. Give instructions that he/she is not to return to work until approval is received from a designated member of the crisis management team.

STEP 9 - The crisis management team should meet to

review and analyze the information collected. If it is determined that the individual is not a threat to self or others, a decision needs to be made concerning a referral for counseling. Should this be on a voluntary basis or as a condition of employment? Should the employee be dismissed because of company policy?

STEP 10 - If the specialist decides the individual is an immediate danger to self or others, decisions need to be made. Should mental health or law enforcement be notified? How will the employee's separation from the company be handled? Is the company's position defensible? Should the company seek a temporary restraining order? What scope and how long should security be enforced?

MANAGEMENT ROLE - EMPLOYEE RELATIONS & POLICIES

Management's most important line of defense in preventing workplace violence is to combine preventive Human Resource practices with close attention to the warning signs for the prediction of violent behavior. A plan should be in place with a management team trained on what to watch for and what procedures to follow. Decide who will evaluate the situation and lead the team and when to refer an employee for counseling. Management must be especially alert for signs of excessive stress. Since disagreement with management has been a part of many incidents of violence, having knowledgeable, effective managers is extremely important. Frederick Ramsey, Director of the State of Maryland Employee Assistance Program, said, "The hardest thing we have to do is convince managers that you have to help people by letting them know that what they are doing is unacceptable."

EMPLOYEE ASSISTANCE PROGRAMS

Most large businesses and corporations have Employee Assistance Programs in place. If not, such a program should be considered. Mental health services are also included in many benefit packages. These services should be available for personal and family problems as well as for on-the-job issues. Management should understand their rights as employer and employees' rights regarding confidentiality.

EMPLOYEE SAFETY

In-service training regarding workplace safety is an integral part of creating a safe environment. Topics can include first aid and CPR training, safety awareness, and personal safety training, as well as training to recognize potentially violent situations in the workplace. Enhancing employee security is one way of letting employees know that management is concerned for their welfare.

HIRING PRACTICES

Part of any plan to prevent workplace violence includes written policies concerning adequate evaluation of the people to be hired. Employers may be legally required to take measures to avoid hiring dangerous people. A tort known as *'negligent hiring'* obligates employers when there is an increased risk of harm by an employee toward a third party. Background investigations to determine the potential risk of hiring dangerous individuals are important.

EMPLOYEE SECURITY

Employers are required by law to provide adequate security. Many court actions have raised questions of negligent security practices as well as the removal of potential hazards. Administrative controls such as requiring that employees not work alone, and conflict resolution training are suggested. This is geared toward controlling violence from customers and clients, but can include disgruntled fellow employees.

As stated previously, management should assess the current level of security and related policy and procedures to make changes that will improve the security of the work environment, both from employees who have been identified as dangerous as well as upset clients, and robbers. Many security consultants are available that can help with an evaluation of a company's workplace.

The written plan for handling violence should include communication with security and its role in each step of the process. Details concerning what will happen before, during and after any incidents should be included.

EMPLOYEE TERMINATIONS

In the current legal climate, sound management practices must be followed when terminations or layoffs occur. Managers must complete the required documentation and follow company procedures or the result could be a lawsuit. Termination and layoff have been the cause of violent reactions in the past. Some general guidelines to help employers handle these delicate situations include:

- Treat all employees with respect and dignity.
- All disciplinary actions should be applied consistently to all employees.
- If possible, adverse actions should be avoided when an employee is pregnant, undergoing divorce, or dealing with critical illness or the recent death of a family member.
- Have another person present when a supervisor delivers the bad news—preferably a Human Resource manager.
- Don't expect discharged or laid-off employees to act rationally.
- Stick to business reasons for the dismissal.

- Be confidential and be honest about the reason for the termination or layoff.
- Except in cases of fraud, theft, or other special circumstances, consider carefully the need to have security personnel present. Allow the employee to come back after-hours to clear out his/her work station.
- Have all forms and written materials regarding benefits, profit-sharing, etc. prepared in advance. Prepare a checklist of property to be accounted for.
- Spend time preparing exactly what you want to say. Be direct, concise, and businesslike.
- Change security codes and computer passwords previously used by discharged employees.

DOWNSIZING

Terminations and layoffs generate a lot of stress. Special considerations should be made when a company is downsizing. The most important is honest communication from management. Employees must believe what they are being told. Job stability is a major factor in people's lives and uncertainty regarding one's future employment can have a significant impact on individuals. Discuss the reasons for the reduction, allow time for questions, and be available in the future to answer additional questions.

Expect employees to be angry. Some will be resentful and attempt to sabotage the employer, or seek other revenge. Security personnel should make a strong presence during this tense time.

It is recommended that employees targeted for downsizing not be notified too far in advance, except in cases requiring adherence to any State or Federal laws. This invites theft, sabotage, and loss of productivity. The bill (Warn Act) recently passed by Congress requiring 60 days advance notice of plant closings and layoffs should be observed.

If more than 25 employees are being dismissed, prepare information for the news media. Also, it is a good idea to have a company representative call discharged employees on a regular basis until they have another job. This shows that the company still cares.

OUTPLACEMENT

Terminations due to takeovers, mergers, and downsizing are on the increase. Many employers provide outplacement services through their own Human Resources department or through an independent firm. Effective outplacement services are in the interest of both the employer and the employee and project the image of a caring employer—both to the terminated employee and to those remaining in the organization. It is a reassuring safety net to individuals in cases of termination or downsizing. Outplacement services can be a strong factor in reducing stress and the possibility of a violent reaction from an employee.

NOTES

CHAPTER 9

TRAINING PROGRAMS AND TRAUMA PLAN

TRAINING PROGRAM

Because of the increase in violent incidents in the workplace, it is important for each company to assess its individual circumstances and develop a plan of action to handle potential problems. This plan should address **prediction** of the problem, **prevention,** which includes training of personnel to handle potentially violent situations, and the potential **trauma** of such situations. An "Alert and Avert" program for an organization must start with education. Education for all employees, but particularly for managers and supervisors, can increase participants' sensitivity to the clues that suggest an employee could become dangerous. Clues that might previously have gone unnoticed or been ignored are suddenly signals to the trained observer to be on the alert, and, most importantly, to alert others.

Such training should begin with an inventory of the behaviors frequently associated with violence. Ideally, the training will not stop there. Providing a "checklist of warning signs" is only the beginning. A thorough education strategy will also deepen participants' understanding and appreciation of the meaning of work to employees. This appreciation will assist them in taking emotional/psychological precautionary steps with employees who are threatened by losses in their work and/or personal lives. Such measures, though subtle and intangible, can be as important as the company's security system.

As well as a policy to handle previously terminated or laid-off employees, a part of an overall plan to handle violent incidents should include training managers and supervisors to observe and report important warning signs of potential violent outbursts. Be aware if employees or co-workers are:
- Showing signs of lowered productivity
- Exhibiting a loss of self-esteem
- Displaying a lack of job satisfaction
- In a position of no growth or opportunity
- Experiencing a major change in financial status

EDUCATION AND COMMUNICATION

The indispensable key to prevention is education and communication, perhaps beginning with communication among workers who too often dismiss as meaningless the muttered threats by fellow workers and who are reluctant to tell management for fear of ostracism. Effective communication between employees and management and personal communication between a supervisor and a potentially dangerous employee are critical. Developing communications links among departments deeply involved in anticipating and averting potential danger, such as Human Resources and Employee Assistance Programs, and other departments is essential.

OPEN COMMUNICATION

Achieving open communication is an ideal, but the ideal is not easily attained. In the workplace there are five inherent barriers to complete open communications.

1. Fear. This barrier has many faces, from fear of physical injury to fear of needlessly compounding the problems of the already suspect employee.

2. Anger. This, too, is multifaceted and applies equally to the employee's anger or the anger of the employee's supervisor at the employee's perceived ineptitude or indifference. A shouting match is not communication.

3. Denial. This is perhaps the most comfortable out, the self-delusion that maybe the problem will go away if it's ignored long enough.

4. Guilt. No rational, compassionate person wants to damage or destroy another person's life, which is an admirable trait. The rationalization, in this case misguided, goes something like this: "Well, the poor guy obviously has enough problems without me adding to them by messing up his personnel file. Anyhow, maybe part of his problem is my fault."

5. Accommodation. This is perhaps a combination of all the other barriers, the one that makes bending the rules preferable to exposing and trying to cope with the real problem. In some cases it even extends to doing the employee's work for him. In most cases it at least involves correcting and even covering up the employee's mistakes.

So, to reach the desired, even required, level of communication, the first and perhaps largest step in recognizing, identifying and, yes, helping a potentially violent employee, barriers must be overcome. The good news is, none of those barriers is insurmountable.

MANAGEMENT RESPONSIBILITY

One thing almost all incidents of workplace violence have in common is that sometime before the emotionally enraged employee reached the breaking point and embarked on a bloody, tragic spree, he/she unfailingly exhibited telltale signs of pending trouble. In all such cases those signs went undetected, unreported, were ignored or, at best, treated lightly. Who is responsible for such glaring oversights? To narrow the field, **everybody.** There's more than enough blame to go around.

EMPLOYEE RESPONSIBILITY

The list includes fellow employees. It is they who are most frequently exposed to the utterances of their enraged co-worker, utterances that may begin as standard gripes but eventually escalate into genuine threats, and from there into what might even be classified as self-fulfilling prophecies. When an employee says, "What happened in Edmond, Oklahoma, could happen here," he has gone well beyond daily griping. It's the kind of remark that should be reported to someone higher up in the chain of command and dealt with immediately. It almost never is reported, however, for various reasons. One is the belief that it is socially unacceptable to be branded a "snitch." Another, almost as inbred, is the barrier between labor and management. A third is the American penchant for giving a person the benefit of the doubt, to dismiss such remarks with, "Well, that's just old Joe letting off steam. He really doesn't mean anything by it."

LACK OF TRAINING

Also to blame is the lack of training for supervisory personnel who are solely focused on productivity and have neither the time nor, more significantly, the inclination to take notice of an employee's personal problems. Unless, of course, those problems affect productivity, in which case the answer all too often is a summons to the employee to a closed-door meeting, during which the employee is advised to "straighten up, or else." Not exactly an enlightened approach, but still a rather basic one even today.

TRAUMA PLAN

Once a company has set policies and procedures in place to train employees, managers and supervisors to be alert and possibly predict and prevent potential violence in the workplace, the next step is to devise a trauma plan in case violence does occur.

In some cases the violence may be caused by a disgruntled worker, a former employee, or a relative of an employee. In others, the violence may be caused by an angry client or customer. Sometimes, the violence is caused by a stranger—as in the case of bank robberies. Regardless, management will be looked to for immediate action.

In the midst of chaos, many important and practical decisions will need to be made. Aside from emergency medical actions and dealing with the police, innumerable problems will need attention. Examples include: calming hysterical witnesses, notifying the victims' families, arranging transportation for employees, repairing phones that are inoperable, processing payroll and personnel information that may be inaccessible or destroyed, cleaningup damaged offices and grounds, and contacting and informing the press. Management needs to take care of the practical considerations so that grieving employees can heal.

Companies must consider how to handle the disruption to their normal business activities. Customer orders may be delayed, someone may have to notify clients of changes in the schedule, etc. Having a trauma plan in place ahead of time will help a company make it through a violent crisis.

COMPONENTS OF THE TRAUMA PLAN

Information to include in a plan is a trauma counselor who can be called to provide immediate help for distressed employees and witnesses. A person can be designated to handle the press. Details such as insurance coverage for medical expenses and transportation for employees should be addressed. Telephone teams should be set up not only to call family members on the day of the incident, but also to advise employees and their families as to available psychotherapy services, when to return to work, etc.

TRAUMA TRAINING PROGRAMS

Trauma response plans should include training programs to increase information about trauma and its psychological impact, as well as preparation of rapid response personnel to assist in crisis intervention and debriefing. They should also include procedures for monitoring individuals during emotional turmoil and recovery phases following trauma so that effective mental health referralS can be made when necessary.

These plans should be proactive and include assessing an employee's potential for violence before an incident occurs, and also reactive for handling a specific crisis. The issues of privacy, labor regulations, and security should be taken into consideration.

THE ROLE OF SECURITY PERSONNEL

The role of security in the aftermath of an event will require special considerations. Immediate security decisions will have to be made. Increased security measures might include the actual presence of additional security personnel, or electronic/mechanical modifications to control physical entry.

Chapter 9

POST-TRAUMATIC STRESS

In the aftermath of a violent incident, the survivors, including those who were injured, those who were targeted but missed, witnesses, co-workers, family members, and other people in the organization, can be emotionally devastated and may suffer from post-traumatic stress. The event so overloads and overwhelms an individual that the psyche's normal coping mechanisms are not able to handle it. For the survivors, the workplace is no longer safe, but has become threatening.

Information on the effects and treatment of post-traumatic stress in the workplace emphasizes the importance of immediate action and early treatment in order to avoid more severe, debilitating responses at a later time. Criteria used to identify post-traumatic stress disorder are:

1. A traumatic event outside the range of ordinary human encounter is experienced.

2. Persistent re-experiencing of reactions associated with the event.

3. An ongoing avoidance of trauma-related stimuli or numbing of psychological responsiveness.

4. Symptoms of increased arousal and elevated anxiety not present before the trauma event, and

5. Duration of these persistent symptoms for at least one month.

Many individuals may not reach the thresholds for a full diagnosis of Post Traumatic Stress Disorder, but may suffer a number of clinical symptoms. Individuals go through three stages of recovery.

The Impact Stage

Depending on the intensity and duration of the trauma, this stage may last from hours to days. Symptoms include chills, nausea, headaches, appetite disturbances, difficulty

127

concentrating, irritability, shock, disbelief, disorientation, affective numbness, emotional suppression, depression, withdrawal, regressive behaviors, sleep disturbances, anxiety and hyper-arousal. Some may turn to increasing use of alcohol and drugs to numb their feelings.

Emotional Turmoil Stage

This stage may last several months or indefinitely. First stage symptoms continue. A wide range of changing feelings including fear, anger, grief, guilt, swings from self-confidence to self-deprecation, and frustration are experienced. A sense of lowered personal control, challenges to interpersonal trust and religious belief, an increased sense of vulnerability, loss of a sense of fairness, struggles with self-blame and an overall sense of personal violation may be experienced. Other difficulties include re-experiencing the trauma (e.g., nightmares, flashbacks, conditioned responses), an increased tendency to avoid trauma-associated stimuli and difficulty tolerating arousal.

Adjustment Stage

During this phase, the individual attempts to gain control over his or her emotional life while reformulating the meaning of the traumatic experience. To return to psychological health, the traumatic event must be processed and integrated into the individual's self-concept and world view.

PERSONAL AND COMPANY LOSS

If the assimilation does not take place, the symptoms may continue and intensify. Insensitivity by the police, emergency responders, media, community agencies, or the employer can further victimize and traumatize the individual already trying to cope with the experience. If management responds slowly or with disinterest or blame, employees may experience feelings of betrayal. Individuals are at risk of ongoing stress reactions, and even rage, if management is perceived as resistant to providing information or taking corrective action.

In a situation like this, decreased productivity is a normal consequence. Time during working hours for debriefing, therapy, informal conversations among employees, and more formal group meetings is important. Management's coping with the emotional impact immediately lets employees know that the employer cares and is involved. When employees feel good about the employer's intervention, and that management is interested in their well-being, loyalty and goodwill toward the company increases. Denying the severity of the incident or the need for therapy will only prolong recovery and lead to a loss of morale and perhaps lawsuits.

Whether the victim was a co-worker or family member, and how directly the individual was impacted by the trauma, are other factors that influence the intensity of the trauma reaction. Pre-existing life stress, personality, management style, family support, history of prior trauma, and coping strategies will also have an effect.

In view of the stresses experienced by those involved in a violent incident in the workplace, a well-thought out plan, informed management, and immediate response are important. Most people report losing a sense of safety and well-being. This can affect a person's entire life, including relationships with family as well as the ability to work and carry out everyday activities.

The overall goals are the decrease of distressing symptoms, the enhancement of emotional expression and the assimilation of the trauma experience for employees. The company trauma team should provide support, reduce self-blame, restore a level of trust and strive to desensitize individuals to incapacitating fears and anxieties. The intervention may be done individually or in groups. Each situation needs careful evaluation and flexibility.

KEEP EMPLOYEES INFORMED
The trauma team should work together with the EAP to keep employees informed. Team members should have the ability to make decisions, should be accessible 24 hours a day and be located in one place to make information dissemination convenient. The more informed and involved employees are, the better support they provide to the company and the more comfortable they are with what has happened.

ACTION AT THE ELGAR CORPORATION
The trauma team used by Elgar Corporation in San Diego worked closely with management and therapists. Therapy was offered to Hansel's wife, since she and her children were victimized.

As a result of the tragic incident many changes occurred at the company. Management agreed with the need for improved communication and the need to improve conditions at the plant. They realized that a gap existed between supervisors and employees, whose perception was that management didn't care, that they were only concerned with profits. A new security system was implemented. Now there's a mechanized identification card system and employees use a card to open doors. Employees and visitors wear badges. An emergency warning system has been installed.

Management at Elgar reports that people still talk about the incident but in a different way. They talk about what kinds of things they can do to become a better company. They feel part of an "Elgar family" and want to make their working environment the best they can. The climate in the company is warmer, more comfortable.

MEMORIALS

Employees at the Elgar Corporation did not forget the two men who died. They collected a memorial fund and formed a committee made up of management and workers and the victims' wives. Both of the victims liked to fly, so the employees set up a scholarship for employees who want to learn to fly, and a plaque to commemorate the grant was planned.

WHAT AN ORGANIZATION CAN DO

An organization has several options open to them concerning intervention measures necessary to curtail and manage workplace violence.

1. Personnel Selection Procedures. Dr. Michael Mantell, who has vast experience in dealing with violence-induced trauma, was among the first asked to assist in the McDonald's massacre in San Ysidro, California. It was at the McDonald's Restaurant, on July 18, 1984, that James O. Huberty killed 21 adults and children. Mantell was also present early on the scene in Edmond, Oklahoma. Mantell believes correct personnel selection procedures are the most effective way to prevent potential problems.

There are two primary ways to assess future employees. The first one is through pre-employment testing. The review of research in the field indicates that workplace violence tendencies can be predicted when standardized testing instruments are used for personnel selection. Popular clinical tests such as the Minnesota Multiphasic Personality Inventory (MMPI), the California Personality Inventory (CPI), Personnel Selection Inventory (PSI) and the Sixteen Personality Factor Questionnaire can predict aggressive behavior and potential violence.

However, certain laws within your state may prevent the use of these instruments. It would be wise to check. For example, the MMPI, a highly effective clinical instrument, has been ruled by a California court as illegal to use because of questions asking about sexual or religious beliefs. Other testing, like the 16PF, does not ask those questions and may be more acceptable in your state. The other prohibitive factor may be cost. Most of these tests require a licensed or certified mental health professional to evaluate the results. The best course of action is to check with several psychological services that provide testing to insure responsiveness and low cost.

The second effective pre-employment screening method is the interview and checking of references. An effective interview has three aspects that are equally critical in assessing a potential candidate. The first aspect is **Competency**. Most companies have little problem assessing the competency level of the potential hire. In fact, most of the time, that is what the hiring manager is most concerned about in the interview process. However, a potentially violent employee can be very skilled. Hansel was recognized for his outstanding electronic skills.

The company hiring manager needs to spend an equal amount of time in two other areas as well: **Character** and **Chemistry**. All companies would like to hire an individual that they can trust concerning their products and services. Integrity, authenticity, genuineness, initiative, and commitment are all by-products of one's character. Chemistry has to do with the ability to get along with others. It has been the author's experience that most individuals fired are terminated because of interpersonal conflict. What are some of the questions that need to be asked? Ask questions that relate to work history. Probe deeply into reasons for leaving an organization and the relationship with co-workers and management. Superficial responses are not acceptable and should be a cause for alarm.

Present hypothetical situations that deal with conflict in the workplace; how does the potential employee respond? Ask the potential employee who was the most difficult person they ever worked for and why? Ask about outside interests? Be careful not to violate legal parameters. What magazines do they like to read? What was the title of the last book they read? Why did they like it? Probe with questions like why, when, where, and with whom? Checking references is very critical. Although previous companies are very reluctant to give anything but dates of employment for your potential employee, there are questions that can be asked. For example, is the individual eligible for rehire? Verify dates and positions. If the references do not list his or her immediate supervisor, find out why. If you are not getting positive responses to your questions, trust your instincts. Eliminating the problem at the beginning can save time, money, and even lives.

2. Supervisory Training. Supervisors should be trained to pay attention to the early warning signs of stress. Supervisors should be tuned in to staff needs. One of the best ways to be tuned in with your staff is "management by observation." Spend time walking around your site interacting with your team. Some educational and training programs recommended to enhance quality intervention are:
- Stress Management
- Effective Communication Seminars
- Conflict Resolution Seminars
- Teambuilding
- Dealing With Difficult People
- Managing Change
- Termination Training

133

3. On-site Support Services. When trouble occurs, immediate response is necessary. Employee assistance professionals should be called to assist the victims. Police should immediately be notified. The first 24 hours following any traumatic incident are critical, especially concerning workplace violence. The Human Resource professional should contact the trauma team immediately after the incident and clear his/her calendar to meet with them. Establish a back-up communication system to reach the outside world. When Larry Hansel went on his murderous rampage, telephone lines within the building had been cut. First calls to the police came from a nearby building. Saving seconds can save lives.

4. Debriefing with Senior Management. Again, immediate action must be taken to clarify priorities, assess damage, and provide a plan of action. The trauma team needs to meet with senior managers and the Human Resource professionals. They need to do a comprehensive assessment of the incident and obtain a description of the participants. Vital to the trauma team are the what, when, where, how, and, if possible, the why. Such information will assist the trauma team in managing the anxiety of the employees and eventual displaced anger toward the company or key managers. They will also do an evaluation of the Human Resource professionals and other management personnel. It's important that there be only one communication source for the trauma team and the organization. If the Human Resource professional is not selected, then choose someone well known in the company for possessing strong interpersonal skills.

5. Employee Debriefing. A confidential meeting within 24 hours with the employees, a meeting that encourages an outpouring of thoughts, feelings, and behaviors of the entire organization, will provide an educational perspective to the employees to help them understand the process and their future emotional responses. When lives are lost to workplace violence, the company can never expect a return to "normal." What it must do is create a new "normal." The past should not be covered up, but it must not be dwelled upon, either.

In the wake of an incident, the company will hear, loud and clear from employees, complaints about many issues management thought didn't exist. Often the employees will simply be expressing displaced anger because of the tragedy. However, all comments need to be heard. And it's going to require more than a suggestion box. Management must respond to employee feedback with tangible behavioral changes that will both make the employees feel management cares and make sense to the corporate goals. Often the requests are minimal in time and dollars. And they'll pay off in the long run in productivity and improved morale.

6. Individual or Group Psychotherapy. This may include family members and may take several months to several years.

7. Media Response. Expect heavy media response. It's very important that the head of the organization respond to the media. If necessary, choose a public relations/media firm to assist in the various nuances of radio and television reporting. At such a time a company needs and wants to be seen in a positive light and heard with a sympathetic ear.

8. Flexibility. A business-as-usual attitude, even a month after a serious incident, is usually unproductive and costly. If the company isn't flexible and understanding, even compassionate, the common result is a dramatic increase in lawsuits, disability claims, and days lost to sick leave. Additionally, there is usually a significant increase in turnover, which many companies naively choose to view as unrelated. Turnover is costly in human and economic terms.

What kind of flexibility should be afforded the trauma team? First, latitude and privacy. Latitude in walking through the facility and interacting with the employees to determine potential trauma, diffuse anger, and minister to grief. Privacy in that several rooms should be reserved for the trauma team so that employees may come without fear or shame. In one case, officials provided trailers outside the facility to allow employees to have time alone.

Another effective step is providing employees opportunities to meet in group settings with spouses, children, and others deeply involved. A clinician should always be present at such gatherings to facilitate the process. In addition, management must be sensitive to the cultural composition of its workforce. One company, aware of the many workers of Asian descent among its workforce, provided Buddhist monks to help those employees. The same company also conducted special meetings with families because they, too, had been traumatized by the incident.

The most successful plans are those that are in place before they're needed, and procedures for dealing with trauma are no exception. Corporations need to understand that traumatic incidents in the workplace are not limited only to violence. The loss of an employee through death, an injury at work, the sense of loss during downsizing are all traumatic and inflict deep psychological scars that have an impact on the corporation. And always in these times the specter of workplace violence looms increasingly large and shows no signs of diminishing.

To re-emphasize a point, every company needs to establish a trauma team in preparation for a possible event, instead of scrambling after the tragedy has occurred. The team of counselors selected can generate good or bad goodwill within an organization. Choose wisely, based on skills, credentials, and experience. Putting together a trauma team is no time to be foolishly frugal. Go after the best.

BE ALERT FOR SIGNS OF STRESS

Another vital part of the preparation process is for the Human Resource professional to meet with senior management, department managers, and key supervisors to review the signs of workplace stress and the signals of depression in their employees. Teaching supervisors to pay attention to the early warning signs will help attune them to the needs of their staff. Instructing them regarding proper termination procedures that are legal and empathetic is also important. They need to know what on-site support services are available to them. Debriefing with senior management ahead will speed the response time in clarifying priorities, assessing damages, and planning a course of action before an incident occurs.

There is absolutely nothing embarrassing about using available outside support, but it's of paramount importance that the Human Resource professional actively and vigorously participate in every step of the program, and that senior management be cooperative.

As grim and depressing as the spiraling statistics on workplace violence are, there are several measures that can be taken to reduce the possibility of tragic incidents. But there is no magic antidote for this kind of burgeoning terrorism, no foolproof formula to eliminate it entirely. It's indigenous to the times and to the human condition. So it's imperative that corporations be prepared to act instantly in the event of tragedy.

NOTES

PART IV

INTERVENTIONS

CHAPTER 10

CARE-FRONTING

HUMAN RESOURCES

In the aftermath of a violent incident in the workplace, no one takes more heat than the beleaguered people working in Human Resources. These departments are commonly overworked and understaffed. Often they don't get enough input from other departments to anticipate and perhaps avert trouble. They must cope with ever-changing, ever-expanding laws, rules and regulations regarding employment. Frequently, they are forced to deliver bad news, and may even become the messenger who is "shot."

The fact is that those who work in Human Resources, unlike those in an Employee Assistance Program, are not generally licensed clinical professionals. Since the workplace has become an arena for venting frustrations, often violently, Human Resources has been saddled with an almost unbearable burden.

If there's one thing that differentiates Human Resource personnel from other departments, it's probably that they are more keenly aware of the indispensable need for communication on all levels, from the mail room to the executive offices. Those in Human Resources eventually and invariably are called upon, sometimes too late, to deal with a "difficult" employee. Many Human Resource professionals have begun to recognize and appreciate the advantages of an approach called "care-fronting" in dealing with a "difficult" employee. "Care-frontation," as opposed to "confrontation," begins with the premise that any "difficult employee" needs **help**, not punishment, regardless of the company's ultimate decision on how to handle the issue. It rests on the principle of respect for the worth of every individual and an unwavering belief in the value (to all concerned) of a supportive intervention.

CARE-FRONTING PRINCIPLES

There are several principles behind the "care-fronting" approach to understanding and dealing with a "difficult" employee. Many of them are based on familiar psychological concepts that have been around a long time. Put simply, they are:

1. Care-fronting Targets Behavioral Issues, Not Personality Traits. If you think the difficult employee's problem stems from some basic personality characteristic, then you are likely to be pessimistic about the possibility of making any significant impact on the problem. However, if you specify the problem as something the employee is saying or doing— the behavior—then there is the basic assumption of the possibility for change. A person's behavior is malleable, changing in reaction to different circumstances. A person's behavior is visible and, therefore, can be observed and monitored.

2. Care-fronting Views People as Developing and Changeable, Not Rigid and Inflexible. It's tempting to assume that someone you perceive as a problem person is always a problem, in all situations, with everyone, and always will be so. Yet people do have a wide range of behaviors. Hopefully, the employee will be willing and able to change the undesirable behavior and become productive in **this** environment. However, if repeated failed attempts make it impractical to continue, care-fronting assumes there is hope for the individual—if not here, then in another environment. If not now, then with time. If not with the resources currently available, then with outside help.

3. Care-fronting Addresses Performance as Interactional and Situational. It's very easy to point the accusing finger at the problem person and assume that the problem is, literally, him or her. However, people behave within a certain situation or set of circumstances. Their behavior is a reaction to the situation as they perceive it. The circumstances surrounding the behavior in question are the key, both to understanding why someone is behaving as he/she is, and to working out what to do about it.

It's not all their fault. Performance problems arise because of the interaction between the person and his/her environment. When there is a perceived problem with someone's behavior, the inclination is to blame the person, but blaming others doesn't solve the problem. Blaming people is also short-sighted. People behave within a context; therefore, their behavior is never the whole story. It's better to assume that the problem results from a closely intertwined mixture of variables in the person and the situation. Recognizing the interaction between the two is the necessary first step to successfully intervening.

INTERVENTION EXAMPLES
Before the specialists—in Human Resource, or in the Employee Assistance Program—can help a troubled or difficult employee and perhaps defuse a potentially explosive situation, the troubled or difficult employee has to be identified. And that, in large part, falls to managers and supervisors. There are five steps to take in handling emotionally enraged employees, and all managers and supervisors should be aware of them:

1. Observation. The single most important thing a Manager/Supervisor can do to be prepared and possibly avert a serious problem early is to simply notice what is going on with the employees under his or her direction. This includes taking heed of changes in the employee's job performance. Paying attention to the sometimes subtle shifts in the employee's mood or relationships with others. It means not accepting unexplained dips in performance, attendance, or personal grooming, without expressing concern. It means staying close to the employee until the situation is corrected. The following hypothetical example illustrates quite different supervisory responses to the warning signals described above:

An Informed Intervention—Steve

Steve supervised eight technicians in a computer manufacturing firm. He was predisposed to noticing changes in his employees' behaviors because they had all been working long hours to meet a production deadline. He knew they were all fatigued, so he stayed particularly alert to their needs. One employee, Joe, had come to work with red eyes several mornings in a row. Steve didn't think anything of it at first. He attributed it to late nights or smog. Later, he saw Joe kicking the copy machine hard when it wouldn't work. Steve immediately confronted Joe about it, but when Joe apologized, Steve let it go. (After all, he had frequently wanted to kick the machine himself.)

Finally, when on a particularly busy day he couldn't find Joe and no one had seen him for a couple of hours, Steve realized that there was a problem. He began to review the signals and to realize that there had been several—none of them strong enough by themselves to cause alarm. Steve talked to Joe, learned that he had been having marital and financial difficulties, and referred him to the EAP for assistance.

An Uninformed Intervention—Paul

Paul had been a supervisor for 20 years in a large Utility District. He knew his 12 long-term employees well, and trusted them to perform. They were all strong performers and worked well independently. However, there had been recent major changes in the regulatory environment, calling into question the once solid sense of job security offered by this industry. When Frank, his longest term employee, asked Paul if his job were in danger, Paul said, "Don't be silly." He slapped Frank on the back and joked that as long as Frank kept buying him beer his position was safe.

Paul thought nothing of it when Frank talked about having a gun and being tempted to "blow off the head of the division chief." He missed other signs, none of which were alarming individually, but which collectively should have raised a red flag.

Frank's wife had been having an affair, and Frank had become increasingly withdrawn from the other employees. When Frank began having attendance problems, Paul wrote him up and gave him some strong language. He said he didn't know, "what the problem was, but your butt is on the line!" Under pressure himself, Paul had little patience for Frank's unprecedented dip in performance. He made his anger and disappointment clear and abruptly ended the conversation in disgust when Frank began giving a litany of excuses that struck Paul as unbelievable.

When their relationship became increasingly alienated, Paul worked harder at filling in for Frank's lack of performance. He documented the problem, but avoided talking with Frank, whose behavior became increasingly secretive, irritable, or withdrawn.

Meanwhile, Frank, consumed with jealousy over his wife's affair, and convinced that Paul was eager to be rid of him, was drinking excessively to suppress his feelings of rejection, fear, and rage. This is a volatile situation that has all the earmarks of a potentially emotionally enraged employee. But the supervisor is not recognizing the emergency of the situation. Will it end in violence?

2. Document. Specify in writing the observable behaviors that are causing concern. Be specific and thorough with details.

Examples:

Effective Documentation - "Involved in frequent disputes with Accounting Department, uses abusive language such as 'fuck you,' slurs his words, has an unsteady gait, giggles inappropriately. Stated to co-workers loudly that the CEO is 'out to get him but is he in for a surprise.'"

Ineffective Documentation - This documentation is not detailed enough. "Hostile to others—has a bad attitude. Comes to work intoxicated. Has a personality problem—appears paranoid." These statements are conclusions. Documentation must describe the behaviors, the acts, that led to the conclusions.

Record the date, time and person(s) present. Write a detailed description of the incident in objective terms. What did you **see**? What did you **hear**? What did the employee **do**?... **say**? The purpose here is three-fold. First, you will need to be specific when you talk to the employee. Second, you may need to provide data to outside helping professionals, and third, without documentation it may be difficult to justify future dismissal decisions. Moreover documentation sharpens one's observation skills.

3. Prepare. Some in human resources and senior management are gifted in presenting information without prior preparation. However, when dealing with an emotionally enraged and potentially violent employee, "flying by the seat of our pants" is not a good idea. Outline your goals in writing before the meeting listing the behavioral issues with already confirmed documented evidence. Write down the potential options and solutions to remedy the problem. Before the meeting, consult with Human Resources to clarify company policies and procedures. It is important that you receive their support before you meet with the employee. Rehearse with them what you will say and how you will say it. Ask them to help you anticipate any possible reactions of the employee. For example, an especially impulsive and explosive employee may need to have security close by before the intervention is to begin. Prepare, prepare, and prepare. You do not want to be caught off guard! Be sure to arrange the meeting where privacy is assured. Do not discuss personality, only job performance.

4. Confront with Caring ("Care-fronting"). Confronting an employee who is exhibiting some or all of the warning signs (Chapter 4) is an important and necessary step in preventing or averting possible violence. However, it cannot be over-emphasized that the **manner** in which this confrontation takes place can either 1) create the possibility of the employee getting needed help **or** 2) actually accelerate the employee's mounting anger and make it more likely that he will become an emotionally enraged employee at some point. An example of how the latter can occur: A manager (who had done some reading about psychology and fancied himself interpersonally savvy) was faced with the task of firing one of his subordinate professional employees. After he had delivered the news, he said, "I'm sure you need to vent. Go ahead." He was surprised when the employee responded with fury. He thought he had done the right thing! Care-fronting means showing a **genuine**

interest and concern for what the employee is feeling. (If it isn't genuine, don't do it—it won't work.)

5. Follow-up. At this point, assuming you have done everything right, you have made proper behavioral observations of the employee, documented those behaviors, consulted and prepared for the intervention, and conducted the intervention in a careful, caring manner. However, this is where most people stop. The process is not over until proper follow-up procedures are followed. After the initial intervention with the employee, it is recommended that you schedule three additional meetings. The first one should be two days after the intervention session to monitor the emotional response of the employee and clarify any points or goals set at the last meeting. The next meeting should be two weeks later in an effort to discuss improvements in job performance made and areas for additional improvement. The goal continues to be encouragement and improvement. The final meeting should be one month after the initial intervention session, if warranted, with appropriate disciplinary action. Like the previous intervention, preparation and documentation is critical.

Those are the do's. There's also a paramount "don't." Don't ignore the problem. It will not go away. Just ask the people in Royal Oak, Michigan.

CARE-FRONTING STEPS FOR MANAGERS AND SUPERVISORS:

1. **Review the care-fronting assumptions.**
   a. The "problem" is behavioral, not a personality problem
   b. The employee has the possibility of improving, that is, changing problem behavior
   c. The problem, at least in part, derives from the employee's life/work situation.

2. **Collect the observations you've made (documented data), and review your documentation.**

3. **Schedule a private time and place to meet with the employee.** Under certain circumstances, you may wish to have an additional person there. (For example, if you want a witness, or if you are concerned the employee may become violent in the meeting.)

4. **Get straight to the point.** Express the concern you have, and provide the examples from your documentation.

5. **Ask the employee for his input.** When the employee talks, **listen** very carefully and ensure that you've heard correctly by re-phrasing what was said. Validate his/her feelings.

6. **Ask the employee what should be done about the behavior.**

7. **Ask how you can help.**

8. **Identify what specific variables** in the employee,

in **you**, and in the employee's environment are interacting to cause the behavior.

9. Identify the specific steps which you and the employee will take to support a change.

10. Set a date for a follow-up meeting to review progress.

Example

An example of how the above steps might actually take place is outlined below:

Art is a supervisor in a paper manufacturing plant. He supervises a team of ten production workers, one of whom is Milton. Art has become concerned that Milton is showing severe signs of stress and that he may have the potential for harming himself or others. He has noticed and documented five of the warning signs.

- **Safety Issues**. Milton had two accidents in three weeks (he'd had none in the previous 15 years).

- **Concentration Problems/Confusion** On three occasions, Art had noticed Milton staring into space. When Art spoke to him, Milton had difficulty re-orienting himself and focusing on what Art was saying.

- **Unusual Behavior**. Milton had suddenly made frequent statements about, "Jesus speaking to him personally" about the country going to hell. He didn't seem to notice when his co-workers reacted to his statements with surprise and asked him questions.

It was as if he was talking **at** them, not to them.

- **Poor Health and Hygiene.** Milton had been coming to work unkempt and with a distinct body odor.

- **Attendance Problems.** Milton had become casual and unconcerned about getting to work on time. He at first gave excuses, but then just shrugged when Art confronted him.

****

Following the steps above, Art started his care-fronting intervention:

- He began by reviewing the assumptions behind care-fronting. He reminded himself that Milton was not a "nut," but that he was demonstrating a change in his behavior, for which there was undoubtedly a reasonable explanation. He thought about Milton's performance in the past, which had been good, and worked to recapture the positive feelings he had once had for Milton. He resolved to make an effort to help Milton insofar as he was able to.

- He started documenting two weeks after he first noticed changes in Milton's behavior. He collected what he had written, supplemented from his memory, and made a list of the actual behaviors that caused him concern. He prepared a brief agenda of how he would approach Milton both before and during the meeting.

- Art approached Milton first thing the next morning and said, "I want to talk with you at

10:00 this morning, Milton—my office will work best." Milton responded in a surly manner that if Art wanted him to meet his quota, he couldn't be sitting in meetings all day. (This said in a loud voice.) Art responded calmly, "See you at 10:00."

- During the meeting, Art begins by saying, "Milton, I'm concerned about the sudden changes I noticed in your performance and work habits. You've been late for work, you've had a couple of accidents, and you seem distracted. None of those are like you, and I am interested in what's going on with you, Milton." He then waits for Milton to respond. Milton squirms in his chair, has a pained expression, looks at the ceiling, and mumbles, "Oh, Christ." (Art does not unload all of his documentation at this point—it would be an unnecessary overkill.) He simply waits patiently for Milton to become comfortable enough to speak openly. Luckily, he eventually does. (If he had said, "Like what?" Art would have responded differently.)

- Milton talks at length about what a mess the world is in, how much he hates traffic in the morning, how he works as hard as he can but doesn't seem to get anywhere, and how he's convinced another co-worker is trying to make him look bad. Art listens without speaking, takes a note or two, and occasionally asks, "What else is bugging you?" He learns that Milton's wife has just lost her job, and that he is feeling hard pressed to pay the bills on his income alone.

Additionally, he learns that Milton's truck was broken into and the stereo stolen. Art recognizes the compounding effects that all of these seemingly unrelated stresses can have. He suspects there might be more, but this is what he has to work with. He says to Milton with genuine empathy, "Milton, you've got a lot on your plate, buddy, I'd feel kind of off-center, too, if all that were going on in my life at once."

- Then he asks Milton what his strategy is for dealing with his problems.

- When Milton says he's not sure what he's going to do, but he has to have his job, Art suggests that he would like to call the EAP in Milton's behalf and set up an appointment. After Milton reluctantly agrees, Art asks for other ways in which he can help.

- Together, Art and Milton develop a list of the things that can be changed by Art, by Milton, and by the two of them in the work environment.

- They create an action plan for what each will do.

- They set a follow-up meeting to review progress.

NOTES

CHAPTER 11

INTERVENTION

INTERVENTION PROCESS

Given the vagaries of human nature, there is no infallible system for divining every potential perpetrator of violence in the workplace. However, there are steps that can be taken to effectively reduce the risk of a tragic and bloody spree by an emotionally enraged employee. Prevention begins with careful observation and continual communication, the most accessible, viable and logical alternative to letting a problem fester. And, as has been pointed out repeatedly, communication involving confrontation will be more effective if it is handled with caring.

Few recent incidents of workplace violence more graphically illustrate the need for guidelines to defuse a potentially tragic incident than the massacre at the Royal Oak Post Office. The situation there had been for many months openly and bitterly confrontational. Accusations had been hurled, threats had been made, complaints had been filed. One of the more common defenses on the part of the employer is that it's infinitely easier now to hire than to fire. Terminating an employee, particularly in a U.S. Post Office, almost routinely involves having to mollify concerned labor unions, and perhaps enduring a lengthy series of grievance hearings. The reaction to the situation at Royal Oak was both belated and ineffective. In retrospect it seems as though it had been tacitly decided that the most inoffensive way to handle the obvious problem was to try to keep the principal adversaries separated, at least in the workplace. What was needed, it's clear now, was someone to step forward to tackle the problem head-on, someone to intervene using the care-fronting approach described earlier.

The intervention session is difficult for both parties, like salary arbitration between a professional baseball player and the team for which he plays. It's possible things will be said, and they often are, by either party or both parties that won't soon be forgotten or forgiven. The stakes in an intervention session can be much more significant than mere money. At stake can be a life, or even several lives. And as charged with emotion as they may be, there are ways to make such meetings more tolerable and successful for both sides.

INTERVENTION PRINCIPLES

A solid first step toward making an intervention session fruitful is to have a clear concept of what it is and what it isn't. What it is, or should be, is an open and frank discussion of an employee's behavior. What it isn't, or shouldn't be, is a court in which the verdict is already in. The purpose of an intervention session is not to punish the employee, but rather to help the employee get back on track, to improve and further develop the employee and, thereby, the employee's productivity. It's counterproductive and eventually perhaps even dangerous to confront the employee in a punitive manner. The intervention session is part of the continuous development process that includes establishing clear expectations with the employee, training, and coaching him or her, and regularly reviewing performance against expectations both formally and informally. The intervention is much more effective if approached from the perspective of developing and helping an employee rather than "disciplining and reprimanding."

TIPS FOR MOTIVATING BEHAVIOR CHANGE

Edward Thorndike, an American research psychologist, formulated the now famous "law of effect" in understanding how behavioral changes can be motivated. The law states, "We do and we behave to achieve those events that are reinforcing for us." As B.F. Skinner states, "The things which make us happy are the things which reinforce us." The law applies to personal motivations as well as motivating others. Problem employees are not without motivation. The problem employee simply has been motivated (operant conditioning) to do the wrong thing. Here are some tips for motivating employees:

1. Clearly state the desired behavior so that the employee understands the expectations. It is very important that the employee clearly understands the expectations. The boundaries of appropriate and inappropriate behavior are often confusing to an emotionally enraged employee.

2. Allow the problem employee to present suggestions to achieve the goals desired so that there is a personal sense of ownership. Making a commitment to change is very difficult, if not impossible, if the employee does not provide personal ideas on how to change. A clear decision to change and expend some effort is critical. The problem employee must believe that he/she can make it happen. That is why input is essential.

3. Begin with reachable behavioral goals that provide immediate success. The best goals, in the beginning, are small and reachable. Successful attempts at achieving the outcome will reduce the employee's anxiety and provide a history of success instead of history of failure.

4. Reward the desired behavior. Positive feedback,

not punishment, has been found to be an effective motivator for long term change. Punishment is only effective when the punisher is present. When the punisher leaves the office, the inappropriate behavior will resume. A classic example is driving on our freeways. Most drivers exceed the 65 miles-per-hour speed limit while driving. However, if a police officer is on the highway, drivers slow down for fear of suffering the punishment of a traffic ticket, only to resume speeding again when the officer is out of sight.

5. Provide immediate reinforcement for positive behavior instead of delaying the reward. Acknowledging the improvement as soon as possible is a powerful motivator. During this period of time, pay less attention to the failures and pay more attention to the positive strides. Verbalize your awareness to the employee of the positive change. Do not spend time with negative items. Remember, changes take time and must be handled one step at a time.

6. Provide consistent regular reinforcement as a reward for positive behavior, then intermittent reinforcement over a period of time. Consistency is the key. In the first few weeks there must be regular reinforcement of positive behavior. This behavior needs to be acknowledged at all follow-up meetings. Provide more follow-up meetings at the beginning, then cut back over time. Once the new behavior has been modeled fairly consistently, then providing occasional reinforcement will be most effective.

7. Provide social reinforcement as a reward for positive behavior. Monetary rewards have their place as a positive reinforcer, especially for those who are in lower salary ranges. Money may not be as effective for senior level management whose salaries exceed basic living expenses. Obviously, there are exceptions. One of the most powerful reinforcement tools is social. Affirmation, acceptance and appreciation in words and deeds help the troubled employee build self-esteem and encourage positive behavior at the workplace.

8. Model the desired positive behavior. It is important that the walk matches the talk. Most employees are very sensitive to the incongruence between management's perspective of how work and social interaction is to be conducted and how management practices do or do not live up to those standards.

No one said there wasn't a lot of effort involved in trying to alleviate a potentially volatile situation. But the rewards for such effort can be immeasurable, not only in what is accomplished—getting a life back on track—but also in what is averted—another tragedy in the workplace.

THE ROLE OF THE EMPLOYER

Every company has the same problem and the same asset: people. Although the primary mission of any organization is productivity through profit and/or service, the means to achieve those goals are imperfect, fallible people. Once an individual is hired by an organization, a psychological bond has been created. The employer expects loyalty. In exchange, the employee receives compensation. Implied in this agreement by the employee is security. The feeling is, "If I do my job correctly, I will be here." Unfortunately, as we know, that is not true. Downsizing, mergers, and acquisitions have reminded us painfully that personal performance is not a guarantee for security.

One of the significant changes that have occurred in our society during the last twenty years is in the family support system. When personal problems mount, it is not unusual for employees to look for support outside of work primarily with their family. Today family support is lacking for many. This is particularly true for the potentially violent employee with a history of fragmented interpersonal relationships. Much of their identity is tied to their vocation and they look at their company as a surrogate family during times of need. This places the Human Resource professional, supervisors, and management in the role of a skilled helper. The employee's cry for help is also a statement of trust, and the company can provide significant assistance to the employee even in a crisis situation. Here are some suggestions to follow during a crisis:

1. Remain calm, kind, and actively present. Your elevated anxiety will only add to an already tense atmosphere created by the employee. Be relaxed, natural and comfortable. Face the employee squarely and maintain good eye contact. Adopt an open posture and occasionally lean toward the employee while you are listening. Listen with your eyes observing the non-verbal signals such as facial expression, bodily behavior, general appearance, and autonomic psychological responses. Focus on the person first, not the problem.

2. Gather information. Identifying and clarifying the immediate problem is critical. Ask questions and allow the employee to tell you the story. Focus primarily on the who, what, when, where, and how, type of questions. Asking "why" questions at this stage is inappropriate. Examples of some questions are:
- When did this happen?
- Tell me what happened.
- How did you respond?
- What is the present situation?
- Where were you at the time?

3. Assess the information. After you have gathered the specific experiences, actions taken, feelings conveyed, and current status, determine what is important to the employee. Look for core messages and themes of the information provided. Assess what is important to the employee and what does he or she want me to understand.

4. Clarify and identify what the employee defines as helpful. Identify exactly what the employee would like you to do. Sometimes it is clear-cut, at other times you will need to probe more. Clarify and prioritize the needs. Repeat back to the employee what you feel he/she is requesting of you. Look for confirmation.

5. Select resources. There are many things you can do to assist your employee. However, realizing your limitations is the key to your success. Perhaps the crisis demands assistance from a mental health professional, or a police officer. Other times the resources can be family members or friends. If your company has an employee assistance program, make that number readily available or have the number of several clinicians in your area who can give quick response. If you believe outside resources are not needed, keep the employee's agenda in focus. Develop a bias toward action and behavioral goals. Do not judge the individual or coerce him/her toward some action.

6. Communicate corporate benefits. Many employees are unaware of all their benefits within the organization. Counseling assistance, emergency leaves-of-absence, insurance coverage for medical or psychological care, chemical dependency programs or number of other services need to be conveyed in an effort to assist the employee. A well-informed management team can save a valuable employee much unnecessary stress.

LEVEL OF DANGER

Any intervention procedures must be balanced with a realization that the employee may be dangerous. It is important to review the profile and warning signs of a potentially violent employee before the intervention. Personal safety must be your primary focus.

ENCOUNTERING AN ANGRY CUSTOMER/CLIENT

Along with the increase in violence in the workplace by a current or former employee, there is also a significant increase in violence by customers. Many companies provide services to the public where routine visits are made by the customer to the places of employment to make payments or register complaints. In many instances a violent situation develops. What can the employee do when facing potentially violent customers? The following steps are recommended:

1. Observe. When there is any outward sign of intoxication, hallucinations, unusual or bizarre speech, Security should be called immediately. Any type of positive intervention at this point would be fruitless. Simply listen to the complaint until assistance arrives.

2. Listen. Customer's need to know you are willing to help them. They need to feel that it is your top priority to solve their particular problem.

3. Avoid Defensiveness. A customer may complain about the quality of service he/she received and you may be, unfortunately, the only representative to whom they are able to air their grievance. To avoid escalating a confrontation, do not defend the actions of your company. There may be excellent reasons why your company took specific actions but this is not the time to provide a defense. The goal is to "hear" the complaint without placing responsibility back on the customer.

4. Acknowledge Their Emotion Through Support. This will reduce the customer's fear and hostility. The customer is expecting a confrontation. Do not provide fuel for their emotion. For example, it would be appropriate to say, "I would like to help. Let's see how we can resolve the problem," or "I can understand how you would be upset, please tell me how we can help you."

5. Avoid An Audience. If there are many customers in the same room, take the angry customer to a private setting. This will serve two purposes. One, the irate customer will feel he/she is receiving special attention, and secondly, you will be able to avoid the psychological ripple effect of agitating other customers who may be on the edge.

6. Establish Boundaries. The customer may make comments to you that have nothing to do with the problem. Calling you inappropriate names is a form of violence. At first, ignore any comments that do not have to do with the problem. Reduce the person's anxiety by keeping to the subject. Explain to the person what you need to assist the individual with his/her problem. At no time would it be appropriate to lash back.

7. Speak Slowly, Softly, and Cearly. Slow down your pattern of speech to reduce the customer's anxiety. Usually the angry customer is talking very fast and his/her entire body is in the fight/flight mode. When you begin to slow down your speech, you will find the customer will begin to slow down as well. This effect will reduce the elevated anxiety.

8. Ask Questions. There is tremendous power in asking

questions. The other person is doing the majority of the talking, yet you are in control. Ask questions that are relevant to the customer's problem, and respond by repeating their answer so they know they are being understood. For example: "Mr. Jones, I can understand why you feel angry. How can we best help you? May I offer some suggestions to solve this problem?"

9. State Consequences. If the individual remains belligerent, step away for a few minutes to regain control and solicit additional help. This may provide the individual some time to calm down and allow you to consult with another employee concerning this situation. If the person persists with threats, inform the individual that you will notify Security unless he/she calms down.

Employees such as receptionists, managers, and supervisors, who are in situations that may be the first to encounter an outraged client, customer, or fellow employee, should be trained in protection. These protective measures can help reduce the tension of the distraught individual.

ADDITIONAL GUIDELINES

- Do not allow the person to sit between you and the door. You must have the ability to exit first and fast.
- Remain seated two to three arms length away. This provides adequate distance from the individual yet provides for effective communication. Don't turn your back.
- Do not have any scissors or other sharp objects on your desk during the intervention.
- If possible, have a second party in the room that is your opposite sex. Often, for example, two males can create a "macho" type atmosphere unwittingly fighting for

verbal territory and power. A third party (in this case, female) can provide another alternative or solution to the impasse.

- Describe the consequences of violent behavior. Example, "If you hurt me, you will end up in jail."

- If you feel you are in danger, Security should be alerted as well as Human Resources.

- If you see a weapon, leave the location as soon as possible. Call for help.

PLAN FOR PROTECTION

1. Establish policies for handling potentially violent situations.
2. Secure a pre-arranged distress signal.
3. Establish conditions and procedures for calling security, county mental health emergency team, and/or police.
4. Outline procedures for notifying employee assistance providers, and medical assistance.
5. Develop a list of potentially violent persons.
6. Provide training for all staff concerning possible trauma incidents.

NOTES

PART V

CONCLUSION

CHAPTER 12

SUMMARY OF PLANS TO PREVENT VIOLENCE IN THE WORKPLACE

CONCLUSION

In summary, due to the increase in violence in places of business, it is wise for every company to have a Violence Prevention and Management Plan in place. Each business should evaluate its physical security policies, its crisis management policies, and develop a plan for preventing and managing potential violence from employees and/or outsiders.

Sound plans include training to identify potential perpetrators and to instruct managers, supervisors, and workers to follow company procedures. Open communication between management and employees is encouraged. Detailed instructions for handling the aftermath of a violent incident and the ensuing trauma and chaos are included. The following are steps taken in the prediction, prevention, and management of violence in the workplace.

PREDICTION

Managers, supervisors, and workers should be trained to identify the profile of potential perpetrators, to recognize individuals under stress, and to practice sound management procedures for hiring, downsizing, or terminations. Managers and supervisors should be taught to observe employee behavior for any warning signs. Workers should be taught to report any threats or indications of potential violence.

COMPONENTS

1. Conduct training to identify potential sources of violence. Familiarize employees with the profile of potential violent perpetrators.
2. Train employees to be alert to warning signs and to avert violence by reporting any threatening remarks or situations.
3. Train employees and management to observe—to know the basic levels of human needs and how to recognize stress.
4. Conduct training of managers/supervisors on hiring, downsizing and termination procedures.
5. If not already in existence, consider establishing an Employee Assistance Program (EAP).

SECURITY PLAN - PREVENTION & PROTECTION AGAINST VIOLENT ACTS

While there is no 100 percent reliable prevention program, the effort to train managers, supervisors and employees to identify potentially violent individuals and to practice open communication is well worth the effort. Many incidents described in this book could have been avoided if threats had been taken seriously. Taking preventive steps will also save the company money by lowering costs immeasurable in lost productivity, damage to corporate image, employee turnover, increased insurance premiums, and potential litigation.

COMPONENTS

1. Define the Company assets that need protection.

2. Establish priorities for providing protection.

3. Develop sound physical security systems—Identify any problem areas—Have written Security Procedures.

4. Assess the organization's capability to respond quickly to workplace violence.

5. Establish written policies so there are clear lines of communication between employees and management concerning veiled threats.

6. Provide training programs and tools for adequate pre-employment screening and potential behavioral problems.

7. Establish written policies concerning terminated or laid-off employees, or when "downsizing."

8. Establish psychiatric resources or outplacement services for former employees.

9. Train managers and supervisors to use Care-fronting and Intervention procedures when dealing with employees.

10. Train all employees in methods of self-protection, both verbal and non-verbal.

TRAUMA PLAN

Just as it is wise for companies to establish management plans to deal with natural disasters, so too is it important to have a trauma plan in place to deal with the chaos of a violent incident in the workplace. Myriad decisions have to be made concerning security, employee reactions, medical emergencies and law enforcement. With a plan in place, the company is forearmed for such an occurrence.

COMPONENTS

1. Form a Crisis Management Team with individuals from Human Resources, Legal, Security, and other departments. This team should include:

- Security personnel to handle immediate security needs such as evacuation or closing the building.
- Emergency Medical procedures—Who to contact

- Emergency Law Enforcement Procedures—Who to contact, etc.
- A professional trauma counselor.

2. Establish a telephone team from Human Resources to call family members and to notify employees of when to return to work, where to find help, etc.

3. Establish a second source of communication, if possible, in case the telephone system should be destroyed.

4. Establish a plan to provide information about trauma and post-traumatic stress. Employees should be kept well informed on what the company is doing to help after a violent incident.

Trauma Plans, identifying all responsible individuals, should be provided to management and kept in more than one place. Important phone numbers should be made available to all managers, supervisors, and appropriate employees.

* * * * *

SUMMARY

While no one likes to accept the fact that violence is increasing in the workplace, many companies recognize the necessity of establishing sound prevention and management plans to offset the potential danger and expense of violent incidents. Hopefully, these plans will help prevent disasters in the workplace and ease healing in cases where a tragedy does occur. Well thought-out plans allow a company, its employees, customers or clients to return to a healthy and productive workplace if violence occurs. The interaction between senior management, Human Resource professionals, and a psychological trauma team will assist in rebuilding the goals and vision of the organization.

REFERENCES

Bachman, R. (1994). Violence and theft in the workplace. Crime and Data Brief: National Crime Victimization Survey, Washington, DC: Bureau of Justice Statistics, U.S. Department of Justice.

Bureau of Labor Statistics. Census of Fatal Occupational Injuries, 1993-1998. Washington, DC: U.S. Department of Labor.

Bureau of Labor Statistics. Fatal Occupational Injuries by Event or Exposure, 1993-1998. Washington, DC: U.S. Department of Labor.

Bureau of Labor Statistics. Occupation and Major Event or Exposure, 1998. Washington, DC: U.S. Department of Labor.

Bureau of Justice Statistics. Sourcebook of Criminal Justice Statistics, 1996. Washington, DC: U.S. Department of Justice.

Caswood, J.S. (1991). On the edge: assessing the violent employees. Security Management. Arlington, VA.

Centers for Disease Control and Prevention. National Institute Occupational Fatalities Surveillance System (NTOF), 1980-1991. Atlanta, GA: U.S. Department of Human and Health Services.

Stuart, P. (1992). Murder on the job. Personnel Journal. Baltimore, MD.

Sygnatur, E.F., & Toscano, G.A. (2000). Work-related homicides. Compensation and Working Conditions, Spring 2000.

U.S. News and World Report, July 1, 1996.

Warchol, Greg (1998). Workplace Violence, 1992-96. Bureau of Justice Statistics Special Report. U.S. Department of Justice, July 1998.

RESOURCES
CRISIS ASSISTANCE

Baron Center, Inc.
S. Anthony Baron, Ph.D., Psy.D.
10299 Scripps Trail, PMB 122
San Diego, CA 92131
(858) 549-0501, (800) 391-4267
Fax: (858) 549-0363, Pager: (858) 493-7888
www.baroncenter.com

CMG Associates
381 Elliot Street, Suite 180L
Newton Upper Falls, MA 02464
(617) 969-7600
(800) 444-7262
www.cmgassociates.com

Crisis Management International, Inc.
Daniel Paulk, Ph.D.
8 Piedmont Center, #420
Atlanta, GA 30305
(800) 274-7470

Riverside Crisis Team
190 Lenox Street
Norwood, MA 02062
(781) 769-8674

American Society for Industrial Security
1625 Prince Street
Alexandria, VA 22314
(703) 519-6200
www.asisonline.org

NATIONAL PSYCHOLOGICAL ASSOCIATIONS

American Psychological Association
750 First Street NE
Washington, DC 20002-4242
(202) 336-5500
www.apa.org

American Association for Marriage and Family Therapy
1133 – 15th Street NW, Suite 300
Washington, DC 20005-2710
(202) 452-0109
www.aamft.org

Society for Human Resource Management
1800 Duke Street
Alexandria, VA 22314
(703) 548-3440
www.shrm.org

NATIONAL VICTIM ADVOCACY ORGANIZATIONS

Mothers Against Drunk Driving (MADD)
511 E. John Carpenter Fwy., #700
Irving, TX 75062
Voice: (214) 744-6233
Fax: (972) 506-7952
Victim Hotline: (800) GET-MADD
www.madd.org

National Crime Prevention Council
1700 K Street NW, 2nd Floor
Washington, DC 20006
(202) 466-6272
www.weprevent.org

NOVA (National Organization for Victim Assistance)
1757 Park Road NW
Washington, DC 20010
(202) 232-6682
www.try-nova.org

National Center for Victims of Crime
2111 Wilson Boulevard, Suite 300
Arlington, VA 22201
(703) 276-2880
www.ncvc.org

Office for Victims of Crime Resource Center
P.O. Box 6000
Rockville, MD 20849-6000
(800) 627-6872

Office for Victims of Crime
810 – 7th Street NW
Washington, DC 20531
(202) 307-5983
www.ojp.usdoj.gov/ovc/

NATIONAL HEADQUARTERS OF SUPPORT ORGANIZATIONS

National School Safety Center
141 Duesenberg Drive, Suite 11
Westlake, CA 91362
(805) 373-9977
www.nssc1.org

176

Index

F

Fear. 122
Fired 62
Fireman's Fund Insurance 61
Flexibility 135
Follow-up 148
Forewarning 22
Freud, Sigmund 90
Farley, Richard 40

G

General Dynamics 57
Guilt 123
Guns 66

H

Handgun 59
Hansel, Larry 18
Health and Hygiene 65
Heightened Anxiety 95
Hierarchy of human needs. 87
Hiring Practices 116
History of Violence 37, 38
Human Behavior 86
Human Resource 55, 97, 141
Huberty, James 131
Harris, , Robert Wayne 29

I

Ignorance 78

Index

Outplacement 119, 111

P

Paranoia 53
Pathological Blamer 41
Paul Calden 61
Performance 143
Perpetrator 99
Personnel Selection 131
Policies 110
Post Traumatic Stress 81, 127
Postal Service 25
Prediction 121, 168
Pressures 53
Prevention, 121, 113
Profile 102 78
Projection 39
Protection 109
Poddar, Prosenjic 39
Post Office, Edmund, Oklahoma
Orange glen
Post Office Royal Oak
Psychology of job loss 96
Psychosis 37
Psychotherapy 135

Index

Pathfinder Publishing of California
3600 Harbor Blvd. # 82
Oxnard, CA 93035
Telephone 800-977-2282   Fax 805.985.3267
Web page: **pathfinderpublishing.com**

If you liked this book please call for price and delivery information on some of our other books:

No Time for Goodbyes, 2nd Edition
When Work Equals Life
Children of the Dome
The Men's Club
In Search of My Husband's Mind
Soldier Under Three Flags
Beyond Sympathy
Injury
Quest For Respect
Managing Your Health Care
Living Creatively With Chronic Illness
Surviving an Auto Accident
When There Are No Words
Packing For The Big Trip
Life With Charly
Losers, Users & Parasites
Sexual Challenges
I Can't Do What
Violence In Our Schools, Hospitals & Public Places
Elite Warriors
Silent Warriors of WWII
Shipwrecks, Smugglers & Maritime Mysteries
Agony and Death On A Gold Rush Steamer
World Of Gene Krupa
Dialogues In Swing
More Dialogues In Swing